The Struggle That Made Me

Kasandra Johnson

Published by Write My Wrongs Co, 2024.

THE STRUGGLE THAT MADE ME

First edition. July 19, 2024.

Written by Kasandra Johnson.

Table of Contents

Introduction

I want to explain why I'm writing this book about my life and the beautiful people God put in it who made me the person I am today. Whether through good experiences or bad, those people helped me learn to appreciate it all. Now it's the beginning of the end. The end of hurt. I plan to leave nothing out, and if I do, well, I'll have to write a part two.

I plan to go on tour and speak at schools about my book. Eventually, maybe Oprah or Gayle King will want to interview me. Maybe even Iyanla Vanzant from *Iyanla, Fix My Life* would like to have a conversation. I love her. I love seeing powerful Black women who have overcome obstacles.

I know I am special, and God chose me to share my testimony. I always questioned God, until one day I realized he wasn't going to put me through anything I couldn't handle. From that point on, I embraced the gift God gave me to be Kasandra Johnson, a little Black girl from Oakland, the Bay Area, the underdogs who overcame institutional oppression on so many levels.

Some of these events in the book may shock you but it's my truth. I have had test after test and challenge after challenge. I have been in predicaments I thought I couldn't get out of. To be honest, I really don't know how I'm standing here today, but it's by the grace of God I can share my story and eventually get my people of color—Black people, African Americans, the real descendants of the first slaves—to wake up and realize we are powerful. We are a special people. We are the first to do a lot of things. This book brings awareness to the generational curse we have suffered. Black people have lived in a society built for them to fail for far too long, the victims of an institutional oppression designed to subdue their true selves. We're distracted from reaching greatness.

In today's society, we live in a world with incredible technology, and social media is everything, which I understand. It's a new day and age. But I often think about my great-great-grandmother and my other ancestors and what they would have read in a book. How satisfying it would have been for me to know what they experienced during their lifetime and what it was like being African American. Even though I can picture the discrimination my ancestors faced, what were those struggles really like? It would've been helpful to know the good things as well. Were they creative? Did they have hobbies? If they took care of kids, what morals and values did they have? Back in Africa, were they kings or queens or warriors? What tribe did we come from? What religious traditions did we keep due to our faith? All these questions remind me why I have a problem with the fact that the white man stripped us of our identities.

When we look at a form and check off our ethnicity, it asks if we identify as Black. Isn't black a color? It's not the name our ancestors gave us. My full name is Ka'Sandra Rennee Ann Johnson, but I know my last name probably comes from some plantation my ancestors worked on. Yes, I am an American, but I'm also African and have Cherokee Indian in my blood.

I have a long story, and I have to be very precise when I tell you guys my life story. I want it to be like a movie. As a matter of fact, I want it to be like a movie or a show, but I have a feeling it might be too long to make a movie out of it. My truth might not be somebody else's truth, so I have to be mindful of how I say things, but at the same time, this is my life. If anybody in this book feels any type of way, they can write their own.

Part I
Welcome to East Oakland

Chapter 1

Nobody asked to be born in this world with drug addicted parents or raised in an inner city where society was set up for them to fail. I was born in Oakland, California on September 3, 1995, at Summit. My mom and dad moved to 35th and Allendale after they had me. I was about nine months old at that time. My mom was about twenty-six years old. She had two older children, my brothers, Greg and Major. Greg was about eleven years older than me, and Major was around five or six at the time. Altogether, my mother had six kids, including my brother Dominic on my father's side. The order of our family: Greg, Dominique, Major, me, Kenny Ray, and the baby, Keshad.

My mom was pregnant with a child before me, and his name was going to be Kenny Ray Junior, which is my little brother's name. Unfortunately, he did not survive because his lungs were not all the way formed, and he was already dead when he came out of my mother's womb. He would have been about a year older than me because my mom got pregnant with me right after he died. My mom's mother, Patricia Ann, died while giving birth to her. My grandmother was only eighteen years old when she died from a blood transfusion. My granny died in labor with my mom. I was told the main cause of her death was Hepatitis C. Also, the hospital gave her some blood that my grandmother was not compatible with.

From my understanding, my granddad, Virgil Owens, was both a Vietnam veteran and a Rolling Stone. Though in and out of my mother's life, he had women who loved him who would also take very good care of my mom, even when he wasn't around. My great-grandmother wound up taking care of my mother, her own children, and her great-nieces and great-nephews. They all grew up as brothers and sisters. Though they happened to be my mom's uncles and aunties, they treated her like the baby of the family. Being the youngest among that older generation made my mom quite mature.

We moved to Sunnyside when I was nine months old. My mom said she remembered because I was walking and talking around eight and a half months. One day, she was sitting at the table watching TV, and my daddy was playing with me. I guess he heard me say a few little words, and he told my mom. She didn't believe him, so my dad turned down the TV, and I said something that sounded like "Kiki." My mama looked at him like he was crazy, and then I screamed. I could talk, really talk, at nine months old, but I had already been walking, and my mom thought it was the cutest thing. She told me I was very advanced for a baby, but I was her only girl, so of course I was faster-minded than the boys.

My mom had issues with drug addiction—crack, to be exact. At that point, she had been in and out of programs since the age of seventeen. She got clean when she was pregnant with her kids, thank God none of us are mentally or physically challenged. I mean, I'm fucked up, but I'm not fucked up from the drugs my mom smoked when she was pregnant with me. She had the strength to not do drugs as much when she had most of her kids.

We lived on Sunnyside until I was about nine. I spent most of my childhood there, and to this day, my family still lives on Sunnyside—92nd to be exact. The time we resided there was bittersweet, especially when all my family stayed in the same apartments. I remember all my cousins coming over, and we'd have water fights. We stayed out until the streetlights came on, riding bikes that didn't have any seats on them. It was a fun little childhood I had on Sunnyside.

We were really living ghetto-fabulous, as we'd say. My granny on my dad side, Sandra K. Toliver, was the manager of the apartment. Everyone respected her. I don't know how, but she was like "that bitch" in a good way a natural born hustler. I'm actually her namesake. My mom and my granny named me mainly because my granny had my mom's back regardless of what my mom and dad were going through at the time, so when I was born, my mom felt it was only right to name me Ka'Sandra. All of my dad's kids' names starts with a "K," with the exception of my oldest brother on my dad's side, Dominic. My dad went to jail around the time Dominic was conceived, and my brother's mom didn't want my dad to be around, I remember us all going to sf to see my older brother and couldn't come in the house. He did make an effort, but eventually we didn't see Dominic much anymore.

My mom and dad got married when I was around three years old. My younger brother, Kenny Ray, was one and a half years younger than me. My mom and dad had their wedding in Vegas and then had another wedding in my great Auntie Louise's backyard. Naturally, it was a ghetto-fabulous wedding, and my parents looked very happy. I remember being the flower girl. I was so mad I had a fake ponytail in my hair, so before the wedding started, my Auntie

Erica told me how cute I was and how cute I looked in my dress after forcing that thing on my head. But as soon as she left, my older brother Major came up to me and teased me about it. He called me "baldheaded," and told me I was ugly. That affected my mood horribly—like I didn't even want to participate in the wedding anymore. In every picture, I had an ugly-ass face while Major was beaming with his little nose and big forehead.

Damn, Major really managed to get on my nerves. I mean, I'm sure I got on his nerves, too. Of course, I wasn't an angel, but he had a habit of always thinking of himself as my dad. And as my brother, he knew the right times to pick on me and beat my ass when I was stubborn as hell. He knew when my mom was going to work and when my dad was drunk asleep. Major used to get me good, but I got him back in a lot of ways, too. I guess he made me the way I am. He taught me to not let anybody hurt you, no matter who they are. So, although Major used to tease me and beat my ass, it was in my best interest in the long run.

My oldest brother, Greg, lived with his dad's side of the family at this point. He was my mom's oldest child, so I didn't have a close relationship with him due to the distance and the age difference. He was also going back-and-forth to prison, even going to juvenile when he was twelve. He became a diabetic at five years old and started taking insulin shots. My mom had him when she was sixteen, and she was lost in the sauce, too young in North Oakland trying to find her way. The first time Greg chose to go live with his dad, my mom got clean.

Major, her next son, was a soldier, the one who took care of her and the one who wiped my mom's tears when she was deep in her addiction and couldn't cry to anybody else. My brother was the one who held her. It was difficult for him as a young boy facing our mom's drug addiction. He saw my mom at her locliff. Being homeless without transportation, sleeping house the house, going shelter to the shelter was hard on him. My brother even told me he saw mama weigh only ninety pounds. Can you believe a mother weighing only ninety pounds? Throughout my mom's addiction, none of her kids were taken by Child Protective Services, thank God. We could have been so easily separated in the foster system, but it was by the grace of God that my mom kept us together.

THE STRUGGLE THAT MADE ME

My mom started smoking when I was around five years old. I remember it was a big shift in our lives. We were already poor and my mom was already dealing with her addiction. I guess when my dad initially came into the picture, they both were happy that my mom was clean, but when my mom started smoking again with my dad, a lot of stuff went downhill. I wouldn't say she was reckless with it this time around, however. She knew she had to be somewhat functional for her family. She always kept a job, and my dad stayed home and watched us kids. Sometimes he would get drunk and fall asleep watching Animal Planet or some weird science show, which really benefited me as I got older. I am really interested in science and animals and history because of my dad for the most part. They were functional addicts and did the best they could do considering their circumstances.

My dad was born in Dallas, Texas in 1971. He moved to Oakland, California from Texas with my granny. She was working on the railroads, which inspired me to become the first Longshoreman woman in my family for the Port of San Francisco in Oakland. Sharing this connection makes me feel like she is me and I am her. After all, I'm named after her. My granny had a bigger vision for her family and wanted more for her son in the same way I want more for my family. I truly believe that our blood runs so deep. I know for a fact that our ancestors were strong and believed in themselves and their people because those same values are instilled in my granny, my dad, and myself. My grandmother, Sandra, was the first black woman who landed in Richmond, California. She had moved to California for a better life for the rest of her family. Later on, she never left my dad and always made sure he was well taken care of. My granny was very attractive as well, and I can imagine my grandfather was very handsome. I never knew him, but I heard his name was Paulo. He was from Dallas and had a great union job when he met my granny. My granny said she was the hothead out of all of her siblings and would get into the most trouble. My grandmother had three kids. My dad was the oldest, then came my auntie, Stephanie Zeno, and then my uncle, Rashad. My dad and my aunt were about three years apart but were nothing alike. My dad was very smart and played basketball. He was kind of quiet and kind of popular but very charming and easy-going. My auntie, on the other hand, was a bad bitch. When I say she was cold I mean she was knocking niggas out. Bitches wouldn't even think about fucking with my auntie because she ran with the OG Sunnyside gangster

Hot Lips and OG Larry. My dad and auntie grew up in Too $hort's area, and I remember my daddy telling me they had parties on Sunnyside and Too $hort used to come. Short Dog was really in the house!

My Auntie Stephanie got kicked out of every school she went to in East Oakland. She was the leader of some type of crew and she basically didn't take any shit, that's all I'm gonna say. Stephanie Zeno was a bad mamma. When I attended Elmhurst where my aunt had gone as well, it felt really good to know Auntie worked in the same classrooms and walked through the same hallways as I did. She was running shit, and so was I. I'm not just saying it like I was the biggest and baddest person at the school because there were some real hitters that went to Elmhurst. Oakland is an underdog city—people don't know how many gems are in Oakland, and I'm definitely one of them. Even Tupac wanted to be from Oakland even though he was born on the East Coast and went to high school in Mill Valley. But shit, even I wanted to believe that so bad. He's from Oakland in my eyes; even he said it.

Stephanie Zeno was nothing to play with. Unfortunately, my auntie was killed in '94 when her daughter was nine months old. At the time, they were at Booker's store on 90th Avenue. Auntie got into it with some women there, and they started fighting one on one. One of the other women was getting her ass whooped by my aunt, and had jumped in and beat up the girl who was fighting. Auntie told her to come fight again, and as my auntie walked up the stairs, the lady pulled out a gun and shot my aunt four times. The woman was charged with manslaughter but only received four to six years in prison. The woman claimed it was self-defense because of my auntie's background, but if you ask me, she should've just walked away. Even if my Auntie did beat her ass, I don't think she deserved to die. My dad always told me I had similar attitude to my auntie. He always told me I didn't take any shit like her and could also fight like her, but based on his stories, I doubt anybody was like my Auntie Stephanie. She was one of the baddest who ever walked these Oakland, California streets.

My Uncle Rashad was the baby—about thirteen years younger than my dad. He also was born on Sunnyside, but none of my granny's kids had the same daddy. My uncle reminded me of Snoop Dogg because he smoked a lot of weed, was skinny, and used to always be funny and rap to us whenever he was in a good mood. He never moved from Sunnyside and was always generous. For Christmas one year, my uncle gave my brother his first PlayStation. Greg was going through a lot at the time and took it. Once my uncle saw Greg again, he must have slapped the fire from his ass, but I didn't feel too bad because I knew how much Major wanted to play games.

A couple of years after mom and dad married, when we were still living on Sunnyside, they had my younger brother Keshad. Keshad was definitely the baby, and he was spoiled but not in the traditional sense. He didn't get every toy he wanted—none of us did—but people were always drawn to him as a kid, and he got a lot of attention. He was the lightest child out all of us, but he was a fat baby, so Major gave him the nickname "fat boy." My little cousin, Davonna, was also a cute child. I remember my mom's cousin Auntie Erica, and her husband, Dave, taking her to all types of beauty pageants and taking professional pictures of her. I have a distinct memory of going next-door and seeing a picture of her face in some type of catalog at the corner store. She was so cute with the most beautiful birthmark on her face. It was so big it covered her whole face when she was a baby. I also remember Davonna having a picture in the store right across the street on Bancroft where they used to always sell watermelon. They had a slideshow every weekend, and I used to love looking out the window or over the balcony to watch.

My older cousin, little Linda, named after my Auntie Linda, was hit by a car on the same street as where my Auntie Stephanie was killed, 90th Avenue. Thank God my cousin Linda recovered quickly! We were born the same year, the air bottom at the Part. During this time, my mom was very close with her family and my dad was very close with his family. However, a couple years after my little brother was born, my mom started smoking crack again, and at this point my granny didn't like to keep up with the apartment, and she whined about letting someone else manage the apartment, so this made a lot of my family move out of Sunnyside Apartments. Three cousins stayed in the apartment with me at the time. I can remember my cousin Darrell and my Auntie Linda best.

Everybody loves my Auntie Linda even though she will curse you out in a heartbeat, she has a very sweet heart. My Auntie Linda's been through cancer more than once, but she's always gone into remission. My Auntie Linda was my granny's sister, The eldest, who was living at the time. I used to love to go to my Auntie Linda house because she had different types of snacks and Pepsi. My Auntie Linda loves Pepsi still today. My Auntie Linda always had her grandkids over at her house, so I played a lot with my cousins. We used to have so much fun together even when we had our arguments and fights. No matter what we still became really close really fast. I was the closest to all my cousins at that point in time, at least on my dad's side. I also have a cousin on my mom's side named Briana. She was in the middle between me and Major, so she was two years older than me.

All my cousins are a little older than me, and eventually they wound up moving out. But at the time our house was the safest place to be, even though my mom and dad were smoking crack. All the parents let the kids come to our house, so everyone was there. When I say "everyone," I mean *everyone.* My cousin, Dashinique, is closest to me in age, and she's on my dad's side.

They would talk badly about my parents just because they were functional addicts. They did borrow money or drugs from people sometimes, but they were inconsistent on paying people back, but that was on them. They didn't have to give them the crack knowing that they didn't have the money at the moment for it. I remember a couple of my cousins selling dope to my mom and my dad on credit and in return they would watch us kids.

Chapter 2

My house was fun. We made the best out of nothing. I had all my brothers around me, and we'd always play, whether it was WWE or cops and robbers, killing roaches or chasing shadows on the wall. No matter what we took care of each other. We didn't start noticing it getting bad until we started to run low on food and had to wait for mom to get home and feed us. She was the only one that came home with cash, tips from a waitress job or whatever job she was working at the time. My dad recycled and had his little pick-up truck doing handiwork here and there with Uncle Don and people around the neighborhood. He worked with this man named Hank fixing houses, painting, and mowing lawns, but whenever he did work, he would get drunk afterward, go to sleep, and didn't want to be bothered. Or he would work to get high. Sometimes my parents would have arguments over how much coke my dad smoked or how much he owed in credit. My dad didn't abuse my mom. Most of their fights pertained to getting high or about money and bills. Some of the arguments were about stupid shit. On rare occasions they were serious.

One time, I remember the door opening and my mom crying hysterically. When she finally ran out the room, she grabbed all her stuff and asked me if I wanted to stay with my dad or go with her. The only person that was up with me was Major, and I remember him sitting at the door crying. He was mad like he wanted to kill my dad, so we both told my mom we were going with her. She put us in the Volkswagen we had at the time, and we drove to somewhere in East Oakland to the top of a hill. I remember my mom parking and then crying for hours while my brother held her and told her that it would be okay.

Throughout the years, my mom and dad had their ups and downs, but they were in a good place despite their drug addiction. Every relationship has its problems but the drugs didn't make it any better. I went to E. Morris Cox Elementary school for kindergarten. My brother was in the fifth grade, and the next year he went to Elmhurst, and I went to Webster with my youngest brother, Ray Ray. We were in a daycare afterschool program called Arroyo Viejo at the recreation center. My mom was on assistance, so they helped her with some of the payments for childcare. Arroyo Viejo was my family. Everybody knew everybody. Ms. Mitchelle and Ms. Leslie were in charge of the daycare with thirty kids a day coming from Webster. On top of that they took care of infants and small toddlers that weren't ready for school yet.

I grew up at Arroyo with this girl named Natasia, who was like my cousin. My Auntie Stephanie Zeno was good friends with her mom, Caroline, and they ran the streets together. Natasia was one of my closest friends, and I got in trouble with her almost all the time. We used to play and laugh and fight. We kicked it off very well as young kids. Even her brother was cool with my brother. They wound up doing some time in juvenile hall together and just happened to have each other's back despite their being from different parts of the hood. They have respect for one another. That's what I respected about East Oakland; we had respect for a certain type of person. I mean, it was grimy, but at the same time West Oakland was smurkish. It's true that East Oakland and West Oakland are different environments even though they're all part of the same city.

My closest brother growing up was Ray Ray because he's much closer in age to me and in grade levels. Everybody always saw us together as Kay Kay and Ray Ray—the first nicknames anybody outside of our family gave us. Miss Mitchelle and Miss Leslie gave us those names, and I occasionally used it personally because it was funny. My different names started getting around because I was fighting with people often. When my name was mentioned to Natasia, she didn't understand who Poodie was, which is what my family would call me sometimes (in addition to Kiki or just Kasandra). I understood the confusion, but at the same time different people develop certain names for you as you get older, but I'll tell you more about that later on in my story.

Despite my mom being on drugs she never made it obvious, so Miss Mitchelle and Miss Leslie weren't concerned about us. My mom handled her business, but we were kind of dirty. My mom wasn't really home often or involved in all of the materialism popular back then, even though she would boost when we were younger. As I got older, she kind of fell off with her drug addiction.

Natasia and I did a lot together. I would go over her house to spend the night, and we would then go to the same school together. Sometimes I would beg my mom to spend the night at her house because it was so fun. I grew very close to her. I started calling her my cousin, and we started running shit at Webster. Our little asses were really having a great time. We wound up joining this group run by a local jazz singer by the name of Frankie Kelly. She also had a local television show, and one time she featured all of the young girls who sang in the group. This was one of the first times I'd actually been on TV. I remember rehearsing and being so nervous I couldn't even talk, but Natasia helped me and practiced with me. We practiced saying anything until we felt like we sounded like those people on TV. It really felt like you're just becoming the artist. This was the beginning of me understanding improv.

Even though I can barely hold a note now, when I was younger I had a decent voice. I could definitely hold my tongue and sing a melody. I remember staying the night with Natasia and rehearsing the songs over and over again with her. I also loved Natasia's mom, Caroline. She cooked the best spaghetti ever! I think eating hers growing up is why my spaghetti is so good now. Caroline also had a lot of children and took care of them all. Natasia and I had similar lives. She was from the 700 block in Oakland, and I was from the 900 block, but it really didn't matter because we were cousins regardless. Even after growing up and growing apart, we still recognize each other and acknowledge one another every time we see each other. She later became interested in doing outreach work, and I wanted to work with kids at Arroyo, but we've been lucky enough to sing jazz songs together at different clubs. I remember going to Perles in San Francisco and Yoshi's in Oakland. It was so dope because she let us pick out different characters or different musicians. I was Ella Fitzgerald and she was Billie Holiday. That experience of understanding with jazz music was about eight years ago, but it was amazing. It really opened my eyes to what real music is and how elegant Black women were back in the Harlem renaissance era, facing post slavery and the women's suffrage movement. I can't imagine what those women went through. I remember we had a big event, and we had to sing in front of City Hall. I was so mad because the band didn't know how to play the song I wanted to sing by Ella Fitzgerald, "A-Tisket, A-Tasket," so I had to sing a different Ella Fitzgerald song that I didn't like. I forgot this song, that's how much I didn't like it.

We'd sing together, dance together, laugh together, play together. I remember when we were chastising this boy because he did something to Natasia at the playground. As soon as he hit her, I hit him. Then he hit me, and she hit him, and we fucked him up. We knew we'd get in trouble with Miss Mitchelle, but we didn't care because we were too busy crying about how we bullied the little boy. We were bad together. It was me and Tasia and Ray Ray and his roll dog, Pookie. Pookie got into everything with everybody. Miss Mitchelle or Miss Leslie didn't play with Pookie. He wanted to be a little follower getting in trouble.

Arroyo Viejo headed basically all of the 90s, 80s, 70s, and some of the 60s. Kids came up to Webster and then went to the after-school program at Arroyo Viejo. We all went to karate classes, and Arroyo Viejo had Easter egg hunts. They also had this program where you could go to the creek with Mr. Kent to go catch tadpoles and collect different rocks and other things like that. I even remember when we celebrated Earth Day. Basically, all of the kids cleaned up the whole park. Sometimes my mom wouldn't pack us any lunch, so Miss Mitchelle or Miss Leslie had to get Mr. Kent to make us some noodles. Mr. Kent had the best noodles. He could literally make them in under three minutes and put them in a cup. To this day nobody makes them like Mr. Kent. I make some pretty good noodles, but Mr. Kent's noodles would beat them.

The CDC was right next to Arroyo Viejo, and that's where special-needs kids would go. I remember trying to communicate with a deaf student in sign language, and he took it the wrong way. He told Miss Sandy and another deaf instructor I was teasing him, and Miss Sandy brought me to her office. She basically tried to scare me half to death, telling me it was wrong and I shouldn't be treating people like that, but at the end of the day, I was just trying to communicate with him, not make fun of him.

There were younger people who worked at Arroyo Viejo who were probably in their late thirties or early forties. I remember we had a show coming up, and my hair was looking so messed up because my mom used to put it in one ponytail on my head all the time, and it would shrivel up by time I got to school. Kids would say, "What is your ponytail, Kasandra?" It was bad enough that my brother called me "bald headed" and teased me, and this made me even more insecure. A woman who worked at Arroyo Viejo felt bad for me and decided to do my hair. I felt so pretty. I wore a blue dress and felt like I was Cinderella, but I was Ella Fitzgerald singing "A-Tisket, A-Tasket."

Frankie Kelly was a very good teacher and she understood elegance. She even taught elegance classes where we learned how to eat with spoons and in forks and be sanitary in the way we clean. She spent all day with us making sure we looked nice and had our hair done. "You know, appearances are everything," she'd say. She told us that when we go on stage nothing matters but how people see you, and that really stuck with me as I got older. Having hand-me-downs and wearing shoes that were too small made me feel insecure, but as I walked on the stage I felt I was Ella Fitzgerald.

Frankie Kelly often showed clips of old jazz musicians singing live. As a young child, I was instilled with knowledge of different jazz musicians. One of my elementary school teachers from Webster, Mr. Winters, also told me a lot about jazz musicians. He even had us sing an alphabet composed of different musicians. Mr. Winters had a lot of old-school rituals. I remember a little bit of the jazz alphabet—mostly *B* is for Billie Holiday. You could tell Mr. Winters was very passionate about real music. He also taught us the difference between a sweet potato and a yam. At the same time, that was really interesting because I thought a yam and the potato were the same thing, but they are not. The thing I most remember from his class is my first crush on a boy named Christian. Christian gave me butterflies with his dark eyes. He was very funny and goofy, a bit of a clown, which I didn't like, but I did like him. Christian was the one of my closest friends and wanted to be with my God sister, Briana Spragens, which I will talk to you more about in this book.

Chapter 3

My brother Major used to have to ride us on his bike about a mile and a half from 90th Avenue to Webster for school. He was late so many days because I was too stubborn or Major was trying to act like he was my daddy. I remember times when we'd block the middle of the street because I was walking too slow or I was messing him up on the handlebars or I was too heavy or I don't listen or any other crazy thing he had to say.

I was the type of person that when I reached that point of stubbornness, we'd both get our asses whooped. "I'm 'bout to sit here until my mama come or my daddy come. And you don't want Mommy to come off of work, Major, 'cause she gonna be hella mad, and my daddy, he gonna put you up against the wall and whoop your ass."

I used to feel so bad for my brother, but then again, I was happy he got his ass whooped, too, because he'd beat my ass while Mom was at work and my daddy was asleep. He'd slap me up in a bad way and try to put me in a closed bin to trap me. I felt like I was about to die—he was suffocating me—it took all my strength to push him off right at the last minute as I was taking my last breath. Major used to play hella hard. I remember another time we were acting like we were in a WWE match, and Major broke Ray Ray's arm trying to do a Jeff Hardy move. Major felt so bad when it happened. Ray Ray yelled at the top of his lungs and his arm looked it like it had popped out of his elbow. I don't know if my brother Major got his ass whooped for that, but I remember the anxiety and fear he had knowing that he was about to get in trouble for breaking our brother's arm. We used to always wrestle and play fight especially when our cousins came over. They were some of the most fun times of my life.

Sunnyside in general included some of the best times, and it's crazy because I never got involved with much shit when I was on Sunnyside. I was too young; I was a little bad ass little girl, but that's about it. Major kept me away from all of the politics as best as he could. I didn't understand it then, but I understand now why he didn't want to take us anywhere around Sunnyside and how after we'd moved from there, he wanted to isolate me as much as he could from all of the other kids. He didn't want anybody to talk to me, and he damaged my self-esteem so I would feel ugly. Now I know I am more than what any man could ever ask for. Major was just protecting me and preparing me at the same time for the cruel world ahead of me, but a lot of people didn't know I was his little sister until later on because he was so protective.

We were less fortunate, so we didn't have the new Jordans on every weekend or fresh clothes. Everybody went off on how people looked back then, and I was a dirty little girl—my hair was very short, and my mom couldn't do it for me. The only time I remember my mom helping me with my hair was when she paid a woman named Rena on Sunnyside to do it. She did my hair every week or every other week, washing it and it blowing it dry. At that point, my hair was actually growing, and I felt pretty and even stopped going out into rain. My hair fell back out later on when I no longer went to Rena, and my mom and my granny started putting perms in my hair. That was one of the worst things they could've done to my hair. I had to change my appearance, and the perm only made my hair fall out more because they didn't know how to take care of it, so I had very low self-esteem issues again due to the texture of my hair.

WWE matches happened whenever Major headed to the pillow. I'll never forget yelling, "He broke your arm, Ray Ray! He broke your arm!" Major was mean, but I guess I made him that way a little bit. He was dealing with a lot for his age. He was really trying to hustle and take care of us, so I guess he had a lot of anger or frustration toward me when we were younger because he was trying so hard to be a young man and figure his way out while trying to raise his two younger siblings and get us to go to school on time. My big brother made shit happen, and he wasn't a bum, like he really kept me put together despite how little money we had. He really tried to stay as fresh as possible. I remember him wiping down his shoes and singing songs because he liked a girl, and let me just say that ever since he was younger he's had charm. I wouldn't say he's attractive because he's ugly to me and has some ugly ways, but he's a beautiful person and he has a beautiful spirit even if the shit he used to do to me was ugly sometimes.

Natasia and I grew apart a little bit after we moved from Sunnyside. Natasia came to my house on 94th, and I remember not listening to my mom while she was getting high, and boy, why did I try to show off in front of my Mama? She must've whooped the fuck out of me. She wasn't playing with Portia, and I could tell she didn't want to, but she was trying her best to get me out of the way, so she could continue to get high. At the time, I really didn't understand what she was getting high off of. I just knew that it wasn't regular weed or cigarettes. Even though my mom got high off of crack, some people knew and some people didn't. Some people cared to leave kid with her and some people didn't, but for the most part, when my mama used to get high off of crack, she used to babysit my friends' and family's kids. My mom would make sure all of the sharp objects were covered. Everybody then ate some food, whether it was beans or rice, at least they ate. My mom could stretch a meal out of anything. She would always check on us every time she hit the pipe because she would get paranoid and needed to see what we were doing and if we were playing too hard or inappropriately. My mom was very aware of what was going on, but at the same time, she was chasing a high, and that's why I really can't be as mad as I was when I was younger. Now I understand that throughout her drug addiction she always made sure the people she loved were safe. Regardless of how high my mama got, my house was the safe house, even with roaches running around the dirty house. My cousins stayed with my mom and dad through their addiction because it would be safe. It really doesn't make sense to me how so many people could bash my mom and dad considering how they took the time out to make sure everyone was safe.

My dad would whip everyone's ass and put us in the corner if we were bad. Nine times out of ten, when he told us to do something and we didn't do it, he would put us in the corner and then talk to us after he got high. I remember a lot of times when my daddy would basically go on a rampage because he got so drunk and he was so fed up with us. One time my little brother Keshad knocked on the door after getting into it with us over a video game. Keshad was very little at the time, but he was the baby, so he was spoiled and very much a crybaby. Major and I were not as spoiled, and Major and Keshad were often repping a set on Sunnyside. Keshad was a bad ass little boy and always got us in trouble and got our asses whooped. Ray Ray was my role dog; he took one for the team one time. We both were sticking newspaper in the heater and pulling the paper out to watch it burn before putting the fire out quickly while my mom was at work and my dad was out somewhere recycling. Somehow my mama found out what we were doing to the newspaper, and she thought Ray Ray had done it on his own. I went with it, and told her that he did do it on his own because I didn't want to get an ass whooping, but really I was the one who started it by telling him to try it out. I just wanted to see how fire would burn, and I crack up every time I tell this story because he took that ass whipping like a straight G. My mom made it extra hard because she has a phobia of fire. Her grandmother's house burned down when she was younger with all her cousins in it, and she always told us not to play with matches or fire and if anything is burning to get water to put it out. Afterward, Ray Ray was so mad at me that I told on him and didn't tell on myself, he didn't talk to me for a whole week, and he waited for Major to come home from Uncle Boo's house to torment me and get all of his lick back, which is fair. I'm not mad—that shit was really funny, though.

My daddy didn't understand how to discipline his kids. He thought if he'd beat us and put us in the corner that we'd understand what he wanted us to understand. I see now why he did the things that he did, but it took me a long time to really understand why he used to take his anger out on his kids. My dad didn't do it very often, but when he did, it was bad. I wouldn't say my daddy *beat us* beat us, but he definitely whooped our asses really hard. Some of the times that he whooped us, it wasn't even for our fights. He whooped us for stupid ass shit. I remember one time my dad got so pissed off because we couldn't find a matching sack. Another time, he was so frustrated with me because I couldn't spell well. I told him my I wrote my "e" backwards, and he got super angry and called me dumb. He told me he knew I could do better, making me feel stupid and insecure, but it also made me want to do better, to push myself and be as smart as possible.

My dad would talk to us sometimes without jumping to whipping our asses, but for the most part, he would only get angrier and angrier every time he thought about why he was lecturing us or we were doing something to fuck up his high. If he didn't have enough money or if my mom didn't bring home enough tips so they could get high, he'd get really angry, as well. I felt bad for Major as he was five years older than me and took the brunt of everything.

At one point, my mom sent me a notice that my oldest brother, Greg, was coming around to live with his dad and my dad's son, Dominique. Before this, Greg lived with his dad, so my closest brother was Major. He was the one I looked up to like a father figure. He was a pain in my ass, but it was definitely for my best interest at the time. Major worked his ass off hustling. I definitely saw him go to school and sell weed, and I've seen him go through different affiliations with friends and gang members because he just was one of those kids who grew up in the last era of the real nutcase STI. The DNI, end of the

M•A•C movement and all of that shit marked the end of the 2000 era, down from the real OG gangsters, the people who moved hood to hood were in our neighborhood. I feel I remember my brother being very close with people that grew up in the 90s, Lil Ron Ron and Leon. Major would always talk about how people he loved were going to jail, and dying. My brother really had a hard life trying to figure out his way. It was bad enough that he didn't know his father and his father didn't want anything to do with him after he was born. When my mom and my dad got together, my dad basically took him in. This provided a father figure for my brother and more family on my dad's side, so Major grew very close to my family, and they never looked at him any different. But from the time Major was born, he was the natural gangster. My mom was with a man named Major before he she had my brother, and he had a store on Cypress and a bachelor's degree. He owned a couple of properties, and he was not to be fucked with back in the day. My mom chose to name my brother Major after his biological father said he did not want him. My mom wound up getting with Big Major when she was very young, and Big Major took care of my mom even though he was an alcoholic. He was a book- and street-smart older man, and my mom felt well protected and taken care of with Big Major, but he started cheating on her and fucking around on her with his other baby mother, and my mama wasn't going for that shit. She told me it was either going to be her or him. My mom was really done when Big Major chose to take my brother to the next bitch's house and didn't answer my mom's phone calls. He wound up getting so drunk, he let my brother play outside by himself. My brother ran into the street after a ball, and he was hit by a 1985 Mustang. Major's face was broken, and they had to reconstruct his mouth because his teeth were broken, too. He had a scar from the top of his forehead to the top of his bottom lip. This all happened when my brother was just two years old. The doctor said the only reason he lived is because he was in shock when it happened. Major is a survivor, and he has a strong story to tell.

I still strongly feel that Major didn't deserve half of the things my dad put him through. My brother tried his best to respect my dad as a man and gave him the opportunity to be a father figure. My dad was great in a lot of ways. He would take us on adventures, and he was good at making a little go a long way with some dry salami chips and a soda. We would be good on our adventures, and we went we damn near everywhere in Oakland—to every park wherever there was a tunnel or a creek, a lake, or a river. We'd go catching crabs or swimming in the marina or fishing. We discovered a lot of different animals and rocks. My dad was so dope when it came down to nature and learning about new things. I really appreciate my dad for spending time with us and showing us how precious life is. Animals, nature, science—my dad was into all of that. It upsets me sometimes because he was so fucking smart. My dad could've been a professor in biology. He was into so much stuff that pertains with the world and how it works. He even knew a little bit of astronomy. This is where I get it from, what's opened my eyes to science and religion and my purpose in life. He taught me how we ended up on earth and all of the elements on the planet that make it so special.

My dad is super smart still today, and if you knew him you would see that, but he has very little common sense sometimes. He'll do the same thing over and over and over, and as time went on and his drinking got worse, his mind started getting worse and he started repeating himself. His addiction to crack and alcohol didn't mix well when he was going through his rough times with my mother. He used to get so mad at my mom sometimes, and my dad used to whoop our asses when they were both getting high. I used to hate my mom for letting my dad whoop us so much. As a mother, how could she let him? I used to cry to her and ask her why she'd let him beat us so often and so hard, and she told me it was because I deserved it and I wasn't listening to him. It took me a long time to forgive my mom. Even to this day I still have feelings about her putting my dad before her kids. Even though she took care of us, I really feel like she was too lost in her addiction and was trying too hard to balance our happiness and my father's.

She wanted to make us *and* him happy, but most importantly she needed her crack, and boy did they enable each other. He needed her to get high. When I was around ten years old, I noticed his behavior was getting worse and worse. He'd tell her to shut the fuck up and would get all up in her face. You could tell my mom was scared, but she acted like she was happy and satisfied because he didn't cheat and he never missed a night away from his family. My mom told me before they got married, he was creepy and bitches would often suck his dick. She even told me my granny knew about one of the nasty bitches that sucked my daddy dick in my granny's house, but at a certain point in their addiction, they only worried about getting high. They didn't care about how we looked or if our hair was cared for. I remember growing up and seeing kids who had nice, decent things. We were less fortunate, and my mom could only get us hand-me-downs at thrift stores. They'd only halfway fit, and that is not okay in my eyes because I felt very dirty and I looked dirty. I was her only daughter, and my mom didn't know how to do hair. She also wasn't materialistic, so I was often teased because my hair wasn't combed or I had to wear four-year-old, passed-down Jordans. Somebody going to the same school as me had the same Jordans but from a newer year, so she teased me. I remember my mom used to come up to my school looking crazy because she was too lost in her addiction. Her feet weren't done and her hair was wrapped up having just been smoking. She probably hadn't even washed her ass, and there she was trying to talk to my teachers about projects. I was really embarrassed, but I still love my mom because she made everything happen for me. If anyone said something to me about her, I was ready to fight them. From the beginning, I always protected my mom no matter how I felt about her. Nobody else could talk shit about my mom.

She suffered from depression, but she was always working and trying to stay above the water. She was basically on and off drugs with my dad who did not make it any better. My mom was clean a couple of times before she met my daddy. My mom and dad grew up as childhood friends, and when they got together, they were clean, but they wound up smoking crack again. My mom got clean when my brother Greg came back into my mom's life, but my parents still wound up falling back into that same habit, even worse off than when they started. My mom was fucked up from the beginning, though. She started smoking crack when she was about thirteen, and my dad started smoking crack at a very young age, as well. I don't blame anybody because I think people are in control of their own actions and can change their own lives, but at the same time my dad's mom was very sick for a time. My grandma thought dealing was a good way for my dad to make some money, but he wasn't disciplined enough to not smoke his own supply. My dad has basically been smoking crack ever since then. He never really stops.

My dad was supposed to be a famous NBA player. He was supposed to be a Hall of Famer. He played against Gary Payton and a couple of other phenomenal basketball legends from East and West Oakland. My father was known to be a Sunnyside brother. Even though he was a drug addict, he was a saucy drug addict and was really respected. He had nice legs and was very handsome. Even today, he is muscular with pretty, brown cat eyes. Kenny Ray has the same eyes as my dad, and I always wished I had their eyes. They're these almond cat shape, and his actual eye color was a light dark brown. They're so pretty. When I was little, I definitely was a daddy's girl. I was daddy's little princess. He used to play with me all the time, and I used to love when he was drunk because he played with me until he got tired. I loved when he acted like he was a dog and would chasing me around the apartment. When he'd catch me, I'd be laughing so hard I couldn't even talk. He used to put me on his shoulders, and even when I was falling over, I would put my hands over his eyes because I was such a daredevil. I felt that protected around my dad.

He also taught me how to fight at an early age, even though Major beat me up enough to where I started trying to whoop his ass back. I became stronger and stronger and he fucked with me less and less, which prepared me for a life living in Oakland. I've never walked out and I don't think I've lost any of them either, but there's been a few where I definitely ate some shit. I can take the heat. I mean, after growing up with my older brother, that shit doesn't faze you.

Anytime I thought about fighting a bitch or anytime I was about to have a fight, I just thought about what I went through with Major. I used to be super stubborn. He damn near would give me black eyes. He really wasn't trying to hurt me most of the time, but I was a type of kid who would get someone back even harder if he did something to me. It really was tit for tat most of the time, and it didn't help my brother and I are both Virgos. His birthday is on the fifteenth of September and my birthday is on the third. He was born in 1990, and I was born in '95.

My brother was into music a lot, and I remember his coming home from school listening to different songs pertaining to growing up in society. He loved listening to Tupac, Mistah F.A.B., and Chris Tha Fifth. I remember my brother working in a barbershop as a sweeper on 90th, and he met a man named Marty who treated him like a nephew. My brother used to be so excited to work in the shop and be a part of that crew. They were making money and had a lot going on for themselves. I really respected them because they told Major what to do right and what to do wrong. A lot of the people my brother would hang out with were much older than him. A lot of my mom's kids are past their time. We old souls can relate to people much older than us.

My brother used to write and freestyle to different instrumentals, and we used to all sit around and try to freestyle and roast each other. It was always fun until somebody talked shit about somebody they shouldn't have. I even remember when Mistah F.A.B. had this big block party at Moses Music and Major had to bring us because my mom was going to work and my daddy was recycling. Major was so mad that he had to bring us, but he really wanted to go, so he didn't have any other choice. We wound up having a great time. I remember Mistah F.A.B. called at my little brother's tankers, and that's what we called him: fat boy. Keshad came up there and asked when surfing would start in the hyphy movement, and all day we were basically lit as fuck. At the time, Major instilled in everyone that he was a little gangster from 900 Sunnyside, and that kid used to do Michael Jackson and Usher moves. Keshad really looked up to Major in a lot of ways because he was so musically inspired. Music is a part of everyone's life in my family. There's no life without music.

I remember when Major was living with my Uncle Boo. He's really my dad's first cousin, but I called him uncle because he was older than me and had a certain status. I actually call most of my dad's first cousins uncle. My Uncle Boo used to take his kids on different adventures, and Major was included in going to a lot of places with them. I used to be so mad that I couldn't go. I don't really know why I wasn't allowed, but now looking back, I think my mom didn't have enough money for all of us to join. Major used his own money to go places with Uncle Boo, even though my uncle paid for most of the things they did. Major still needed food and used his own money for that. One time they went to Universal Studios and used a big blue sign to make a video of them acting like Usher in the "Let It Burn" video. It was so cute because Keshad thought that was really their video. He thought they really sung "Let It Burn." Keshad heard that song every day for about seven months and had the lyrics down. He basically thought he was Michael Jackson and Usher. Later on he thought he was Chris Brown, especially having lighter skin. It didn't help that everybody told him that he looked like Chris Brown, too. I guess everybody looked up to Major. We used to wait for him to come home from Sunnyside when we were living on Walnut, and we'd all look up music videos. Major would get so animated when it came to music, and I believe this is why I am the way I am. I mean, he was born in 1990, and all of the best R&B and rap songs came from basically 2000 to 2010. Anytime a new artist dropped an album, Major repeated the songs over and over again, especially the ones he really liked.

Chapter 4

We still see each other here and there every now and then, but we really lost contact when I moved to West Oakland. I will explain that a little later on in the story. In third grade we were in Miss Clark's class at Webster, and Clark looked like a God damn clown. She had makeup all over her face every day. She would wear gloves, and her mom would come to visit, and she would treat us with gummies and popcorn—all types of snacks. I loved Miss Clark's clown-looking ass. She even talked really weird and always wore that dry red lipstick. She was very sweet when she wanted to be and her mom was, too. Once, I lied to her about my oldest brother graduating from Yale university. I know she thought, "This little girl is saying a damn lie," but that's how badly I wanted somebody in my family to go to college. I have some cousins on my mom's side who went to college, like Roslyn and my Auntie Tisha graduated from Spelman, but nobody from my immediate family had accomplished anything yet at this point. I wanted somebody like my brother to be in school. I really wanted to be smart. I wanted to be better than all of the other kids in the class. I think all of my teachers told me that I was special or that I had a gift, and that made me feel really good, especially after everything I'd gone through. I love when somebody first meets me and they really get to know I'm a dope-ass person even with some of the stuff that I've been facing in my life. I really felt that with different teachers I'd had and how they expressed I was special after they seen the type of person I was.

I started getting little butterflies and feelings for boys when I was around seven or eight years old. I had a little crush on Christian, but with Christian it wasn't anything like the butterflies I felt for this little Mexican boy named Sebastian. I had the biggest crush on Sebastian, and nobody knew. I was one of those little girls that liked to mess with everybody, including him. I was kind of like Helga in "Hey Arnold," but prettier, but I found out that Sebastian liked the big booty Bri. That's what everybody called Briana in my class because she had one of the fattest asses in the school. All the little boys liked Briana for her booty. She wasn't ugly or anything; she just had a big-ass booty, the type bitches try to buy today. Bri had it naturally, and she definitely got it from her mama, my godmother Shaunetta Holmes. I won't lie: I was really mad that Sebastian looked at me as just his class partner and not as somebody he liked. Throughout my Webster childhood, I definitely was a bit mean to her, but even though Briana wasn't a fighter, she still stood up for herself. She didn't let anyone talk too much shit about her, but it wasn't until people put their hands on her that she'd do what she had to do. But even then, it wasn't in her nature to be evil or retaliatory. She was the type to ask if you're tripping. She'd be like, "You done? Are you cool now? Because I wanna go outside and have fun," or go to recess or some shit. She was nonchalant about a lot of shit, and even to this day, she's very chill. I love that about her, but at the same time, I hated how it took all of that for her to fight back. I told her all the time that if you don't step up for yourself, somebody is going to run all over you. This was even before Briana and I became came best friends. I definitely gave her hell, and she was unbothered by it. It wasn't until somebody tried to bully me that I realized that shit really isn't cool. The only difference between my bullying somebody and somebody's bullying me was that afterward they didn't tease me or try to bully me again. I would get really mad, maybe even cry, and then beat the fuck out of them and go crazy. It really wasn't in me to be a punk due to the trauma Major had already put me through. It really prepared me for the journey of basically fighting my way out of West Oakland.

Before we moved to 94th, we stayed on Sunnyside until I was about nine years old. Sunnyside started fading away slowly but surely. All my family started moving out and other people started moving in. My granny moved in with her new husband, Billy. My granny only involved herself with men with some money. Billy had money. He owned a care home, and my granny helped take care of the men by cooking and cleaning. Billy later drowned when the current took him while he was fishing, but before he died, he paid off my granny's PT Cruiser. My Auntie Linda moved to 98th with my other auntie, Katie. There are only three sisters left out of my great grandmother Katherine Bolden's kids with Joe Johnson. My cousin, Darrell, Auntie Linda's son, had two daughters with my mom's cousin, which made me them cousins on both sides of my family. They moved somewhere in The Valley, but before they moved, we were the only ones left on Sunnyside that were family. However, everybody was family on 90th.

I remember a girl downstairs named Chelea. She moved into apartment number two or one with her mom. I also remember Chelea having a sleepover and my mom letting me go downstairs to join. She had a really nice party, and her mom made sure she had everything. Generally, my mom did not like me going over anybody's house, even if it was just downstairs, but I really wanted to go, so mom told me I could take some pajamas. I remember vividly packing up all my little things: two pairs of underwear, some underclothes, a toothbrush, and a towel. When I went downstairs, everybody was having a good time and playing. I was making some type of bracelet in the living room when it was time for us to go to sleep. I had to get my backpack to change, but when I walked in the room, they were all playing with my underwear that had holes in them.

I ran up to the girl and snatched my underwear before putting it back in my bag. I felt really embarrassed. Even though my underwear was clean, they still had holes in them, and the experience made me feel poor. Shelly made me feel especially bad because I was less fortunate, and I don't think she understood how less fortunate I was. I wanted to go home after that, but instead I went in the bathroom and changed my clothes before basically isolating myself to go to sleep. I could never forget how that made me feel when I went through at that party. It didn't seem like they were trying to tease me, but little things like that are what made me very insecure as a child.

There were others who lived in the neighboring apartments after my extended family moved. One was Smoky who lived with his daughter named Kimmy who went by Vivi. I was six years old at the time, and Vivi was about nine or ten. I remember they took me to church one time, and when the preacher asked me who the king of salvation is, my dumbass went up there and said Nat King Cole. I was that into music and jazz. It was the type of church where we took quizzes and had lessons on the Bible, and the preacher would call on children to guess the answer.

I also remember a gay couple as neighbors, Peewee and Tyrone. They're responsible for giving us roaches, and we could not get rid of them. They were completely out of control. I hate fucking roaches to this day; they're one of the nastiest bugs to me. The motherfucking roaches fucked with me, I swear. They would wait until we went to sleep to have a party, and when we'd turn on the light, the motherfuckers would get spooked and scatter. I hated walking into the kitchen late at night, especially if food was left out, because I knew they'd be there partying. I would have to wait until the morning to venture out when I could see the motherfuckers and know what was going on.

THE STRUGGLE THAT MADE ME

There were some Samoans who lived across the street and were hella cool. I grew up with their daughter named Deppie. She had a beautiful soul and was very sweet even though Samoans don't play that shit. She had an uncle named Barry who could climb a tree with his bare hands like a motherfucking gorilla. You couldn't fuck with Barry or cuss in front of him because if you did, there'd be a rude awakening. He had a lot of respect for his family, and they were basically our cousins. They really had our back. They had a big ass family, and they added on rooms to the house for everyone. That was so tight to me. Black people they never do shit like that. We are always expected to do things for ourselves instead of putting all our money together and living under one roof. Black people are too damn stubborn, and they're too damn prideful to help each other out. Not *all* Black people, of course, but the Samoans really taught me that family sticks together. They would have feasts with a whole pig with an apple in its mouth and the tail curled up, and I remember taking a piece of the pig's ass. That was the best ham I've ever tasted.

On Sunnyside, everybody was like family, and there was always some crazy shit going on. I remember my mom and dad's close friend from Oakland, who I referred to as an uncle, got into a shoot-out in front of the apartments. We were right there—it was so crazy. None of the kids got shot, but my Uncle Juan was shot in the head. I didn't see him for a very long time after that. I didn't know if he was seriously hurt or what. It definitely traumatized me. It was an eerie feeling to see that happen. My uncle was talking to somebody seated in a driver's seat, and as he got closer and closer to the car, I could see a gun behind his back. He started shooting and the other guy did, too. My uncle ran down the street to 92nd. I don't know what that shit was about, but I do remember my daddy shielding me at the time. This woman, Elena, was in the car, and I could hear this bitch start laughing when everyone else was screaming, "Oh my God! Oh my God!" That bitch had no sense.

We had a couple of fights on Sunnyside also, but not too many. As a kid, I would get into little fights with people but nothing too serious. I remember mostly getting into it with my brothers and getting our ass whooped because we'd fight each other all the time. However, my brother Major would get into a lot of different fights with other kids. One time some kids were playing with paintball in the other apartments, and they almost shot me in the eye. My brother was so mad he ran outside, and the boy who was responsible acted like he didn't do it. I was young, so the memory's hazy, but I remember Major was hella mad and cussed them out. Major also had a fight with this boy once. He lived in our apartment building, and he was trying to bully my brother, and my brother wasn't having it. Major got the best of him at the end of the day and got the kid to respect him. After the fight, I had to put an ice pack on my brother's cheeks. Even though my dad would discipline my brother on a level I didn't agree with, he didn't like Major fighting and told him to not be a punk. My dad used to whip his ass and try to pump fear into Major, but that only made him fearless.

At this time, Keshad was still a baby and Ray Ray was trying to catch a big fish in the dirty driveway that had collected a pool of nasty water by the garbage can. Kenny Ray loved to fish ever since he was a baby. He came out damn near came out of the womb walking like a crab—he didn't even crawl. He thought he was a wild animal when he was a little boy. I don't know if my daddy interest in nature rubbed off on him or what, but that kid thought he was a different type of species. He used to do this thing with his back where his bones would stick all the way up like a fucking cheetah or other type of cat. My brother was a little special and had to redo a grade at Webster because he was so bad. After some shit with Pookie, he wound up going to the new school next door called Encompass Academy.

The principal at Encompass Academy had to take extra time to help Ray Ray because he was going down the wrong path. His teachers saw all of his potential, how willing he was to learn, and how interested he was about science and animals. The next year he enrolled as the first kid at Encompass Kids Academy. Pookie continued to go to Webster and get in trouble. You definitely could tell the difference in Kenny behavior when my parents chose to put him in Encompass Academy. Webster was right next door, and though the schools were on the same campus, it was such a dramatic change for Ray Ray's attitude. He was so excited to go to school and learn. He would come home and sing songs about a caterpillar transforming into a butterfly. His teachers Miss Wen and Miss Z really loved my brother and would have meetings with my mom by coming to the house. My mom had to be on point when they got there because she didn't want to appear sick at all. Even counselors I'd spoken to in middle school and high school warned me not to tell them about my mom's drug addiction. She made me feel so bad every time I would ask her about getting clean or getting some more help. She would tell me, "Oh, you want your brother to be given to the white man, huh? That's what you wanna do? I bet you wish you didn't have this crack-headed, twisted-face mama." Honestly, I don't know what my life would be like if I'd told CPS or a counselor or a teacher about my parents, however, I wanted to tell on them so many times. I wanted to tell people that my mom and dad were sick and we needed help, but I was so scared that we'd be taken away from them. I thought about it so many times, like maybe that is what we needed, but then again, I didn't want my brothers to be separated at all. This angered me and made feel alone. I bottled up my feelings pray that my parents got help eventually I knew Major could handle it, but I really didn't want Keshad or Ray Ray to go through that. I knew they needed Mama; I knew I needed Mama regardless of her drug addiction. I didn't really know her any other way at this point. Major told me stories about when she was clean for a time, but I honestly remember her being high all my life. Maybe in the beginning when we first moved to Sunnyside it was better, but it shifted right after that, and I don't remember Mama being sober until I was twenty-six years old. Even though I'm sure she was clean at points or trying to be, I really couldn't tell.

Chapter 5

I didn't officially find out my mom was smoking crack until I was eleven years old when we lived on Walnut. My older cousin Johnisa was walking to the store and my mom asked her to get her something. Johnisa was angry and told me my mom was smoking crack. My Uncle Rashad always knew that she smoked, too, but he never told me what exactly. When those words came out of my cousin's mouth, my heart was crushed. I really didn't want to know my mom was on crack. I knew she was going through it, but I didn't know it was addiction. Finally, everything made sense, from the mood swings to the reason why we didn't have a lot of money to the reason why we were getting our asses whooped to the reason why my mama's face was twisted and she couldn't talk. I was always wondering why, but I thought she was just getting drunk because every time she drank, she'd look like that.

One day on Sunnyside, my cousins, brothers, and I were all playing in the house, and my mom came out of the room hella high, like she'd just hit the pipe. I didn't know what she was on at the time, but I remember walking up the stairs smiling because I was in a goofy mood. I asked her, "What is wrong with your face? Why is it all twisted and sideways?" I made the same pretzel face she had. One side of her face looked like it was paralyzed or like she'd had a seizure or something, and as soon as I said that I think she thought I knew she was getting high. My mama whooped my ass. She must've sobered up so quick, it wasn't even funny. I fucked her whole high up, I guess. She thought I was trying to be funny, but I honestly just wanted to know why her face was sideways like that. It wasn't until my cousin told me at age eleven that every little piece fell into place. All that time, I thought my mom was getting drunk, but it was crack. From that point on, I changed. I was not her Kiki Pooh no more. I didn't want to be helpful; I didn't want to be empathetic with her. I started to understand why I was treated the way I was by her, and it wasn't because she wasn't a good mom. It was because she could only be the best mom possible when she wasn't smoking and sick. She wasn't my mom when she was high. I wound up learning how to take advantage of the fact that she was high. It was my way of escaping and doing whatever I wanted to do. When my mom was high, I could get away with murder, so I knew her ins and outs. But when she was sober, she'd try to make up for all the time she wasn't paying attention to me while high. My parents punished me to try to control me, but the second they got high again, I'd go back out partying.

When my dad got high, he would be really quiet. I'm talking *super* quiet. He wouldn't say shit; he would just touch his nipples and give them a tweak. He'd have this grin on his face and would sometimes even fold his lips up. The only time my daddy would talk was when he was drunk. He would talk about the same thing over and over and over and over and over again, but no one could ever understand what he was saying. And if you looked like you didn't understand, that'd piss him off more. He'd either put me in a corner or whoop my ass, or he'd do both. My brothers and I weren't beaten every day; we weren't even beaten every other day. It was just random times where we'd get our asses whooped for stupid shit because my parents simply wanted to go in their room and get high in peace. There wasn't a schedule for certain types of chores we had to do, so they would pile up, and my parents would have my brother clean up the whole house before he could go outside and be a hoodlum. Major was good at making something look nice. That kid would wipe down the tables, sweep, do the dishes, and in the end, the house really did look clean. One time when my mom was leaving for work, the house was a mess, so she said, "Major, I swear to God if this house ain't clean by time I get home, you ain't going outside." Major already had a lot of shit going on in the 90s with his friends, so he used to frantically clean up. He'd force me to help sometimes, but if I was going too slow, he'd tease me or hit me. He understood later on that it was better to get on my good side, especially if I knew Mama or my Daddy were there because I would take advantage of him. But when Mama and Daddy were gone, he would beat my ass and torture me if I didn't listen to him. One time we got into it, and I told him I hated his bitch ass. He said, "Yeah? You wanna curse and call me a bitch this and bitch that?" Then he pinned my little ass up, which was very hard to do, and put some soap in my mouth. This only made me angrier, so I started spitting out the soap on him. He must have slapped the dog shit out of me for spitting on him. He damn near spit on me, too, but he didn't mean to do that at the time.

My oldest brother Greg was in and out of my life. He went to juvenile hall for the first time at thirteen and went to prison about five times throughout my life, but every time he came home, I'd be so happy to see him. Greg made everything better. He didn't mind cleaning up, and he was very pleasant and kind of crazy in a fun way. He's been a diabetic ever since he was five years old, so he could get really sick. Sometimes, he just didn't give a fuck and wanted to eat all the sweets even though they were bad for him. One time we had to take him to the hospital because his blood sugar was 500. He almost died so many times. Anytime he wanted to get out of jail, he would make himself sick, so he could go to the hospital, or he'd already be going to the hospital because he did some out-of-pocket shit, so he wouldn't have to go to jail. He used his sickness as a shield, which was not very smart. It's bad to put your body through all of those things, but he knew how to manipulate people when he needed to. But Greg also was a soft, loving person. He was so kind and he would do anything for you as long as you were solid to him.

I love my big brother so much, and the women that he dated were good women most of time, too. I remember one girlfriend in particular. She turned into the closest big sister or auntie I could ever have. Her name was Mika. She had two daughters at the time, Britney and Beyoncé, and they lived with their cousins and great aunt. They lived about two miles away from us, and we used to walk to each other's houses, go to the park, play, or just spend time with each other. Britney, my cousin Christine, and I hit it off so well. Britney was a hothead and loved to fight, so we used to play fight all the time. That bitch definitely got me good. I never really liked to fight unless I was forced to, but Britney was the type who loves to play fight all the time, so she made me a fighter more and more. We used to get serious and really fight. We both knew we had hands, and we both respected each other. We used to challenge each other's strength and fight with Curtis. Britney, Christine, and I also had a little singing group, so we used to get together and sing songs. We even wrote a song called "Butterflies," and the song started like this:

"I seen you from across the way. I don't know why, but my life changed that day. All I could think was I had to know you. You had to know me. Let's get together, so I can show you I have butterflies. I could tell it was real. I look in your eyes. In the back, I feel I have butterflies. I could tell it was real when you kissed me. When you touched me. The way I feel you take me to your crib. We were all alone. I could tell by your emotions that can read it your tone, and I said come on you see how you're doing. I said come on..."

THE STRUGGLE THAT MADE ME

Who did we think we were? TLC, SWV, or maybe Destiny's Child? I really felt safe around those people. I really felt like they had my back. They were hella close to me, and we wound up going to the same school at Elmhurst until Britney went to Alliance when they started splitting up the schools, so kids could work better. At this time, Britney was my role dog. I mean we did a lot together. She was a little older than me, but I was mature, so we matched perfectly. Even though she had her own set of friends and I had my own set of friends at Elmhurst, we always made sure to check on each other and make sure we were okay.

At one time, my cousin and I were getting into a couple of fights with bitches from Alliance. Britney was in this game called "militant girls solid," and of course being her cousin, I joined not knowing what it was. I just knew that guy was down with my cousin, and whatever she was on, I was on. We had two different schedules, so it was kind of hard to keep up with each other. She was going through her shit and I was going through mine, but she was always my cousin.

Her mother Mika who was with my brother Greg at the time knew how to sing really well. One time we were having a karaoke night, and she sung Mary J. Blige to my brother, and he was so juiced. At that time, my brother was figuring himself out, and I think Mika really held him down despite everything they were going through together. Britney had an older cousin named Christine who had the most beautiful, hazel brown eyes. Christine was really into art, and I was very intrigued by that. She was quiet, and you could tell she'd been through a lot as well. Her cousin Curtis was total opposite of Christine. She was skinny, and Curtis had smooth, dark skin.

We used to be so fucking funny together, and we had a ball just enjoying each other's company. Later on, Britney and I grew apart, but before we grew apart, we used to sneak out to little parties. One time when my cousin was living on 89th by Castlemont, we snuck out to a party by some apartments near Booker's Store, and we had a good time that night. Back then, we were between the hyphy movement and "working," and anyone from Oakland knows that working is where twerking comes from. The whole objective was to work somebody and break the boys. They couldn't handle Lil Poody. I was too much for that even. Other dancers were trying to double team me by trying to slide my leg over and trip me, but I was going crazy. I used to really know how to dance hella good. After the party, we had to sneak back into the house but before we did, we ran into a man walking on the street. He tried to stop us, but we kept going. As we got further and further away, the man was like, "You come here! Not the short one, the tall skinny one. Come here! You hella cute!" I was so nervous, I didn't know what to say, but I knew I wanted him to leave me alone. Britney started laughing after I told him I wasn't ready for him.

My cousin Britney and I grew apart when I moved to West Oakland, but we'd try to keep in touch with each other. Unfortunately, we both had too much shit we were dealing with. I also was in a choir with my cousin Britney. Rhonda Benin was the instructor, and she was a jazz and blues singer. She once took us to San Francisco Inn where we watched her perform. It was so beautiful. Out of all my counselors, teachers, and therapists, Miss Rhonda was the only one I told about my parents' addiction. She'd noticed something and asked what was going on with me. I think I must've been not paying attention that day in class, and that wasn't like me. I loved learning about music; I loved learning about history; I loved learning about our ancestors and how they were the first ones to create music with the drum. I was going through a lot at home, and I think I must've acted like it. She took me outside to talk, and at first, I was very defensive. I didn't want to talk to her at all, but she knew something was really bothering me. She just kept talking to me and telling me that I wasn't acting like myself, that I had a lot of potential. She really was concerned about what I was going through, so I told her my mom was on crack. Tears started pouring out my eyes, and I couldn't stop crying. She held me so tight. I really needed that hug. I told her about everything, and she listened. I told her I was scared my brothers would be taken away from me, and she saw how passionate I was about my them. She believed I was strong enough to overcome everything I'd been through.

From that day forward, Miss Rhonda had a different outlook on me. She was really gentle with me and patient. She took me to lunch outside of school and even made sure I had a couple of dollars in my pocket. I remember when Miss Rhonda had to drop me off at home from her show at the San Francisco Inn, and she asked if she could come with me into the house. I told her I didn't want her to go, so she met my mom without going inside. My mom at the time was drunk and high. She didn't know what time Rhonda was coming, so I'm sure she got high but not too high to where it would be noticeable. My mom never knew that Miss Rhonda was aware she was on drugs because Rhonda still gave her respect. That's what I loved about her.

Chapter 6

At Elmhurst, I was a big ass bully. I was doing way too much. I was a class clown and a teachers' pet at the same time. I was so smart and competitive, but I was troublesome and really wanted attention, so I fucked with everybody that let me fuck with them. And if someone fucked with me, I was definitely going to fuck with them back even harder.

Y'all remember when Tyler perry made that movie, and he was talking to Dr. Phil? Dr. Phil asked, "Well why do you think you have to get them get them get them?" and Madea was like, "Because if they got me got me got me, then I'm gonna have to get them get them get them." That's how I felt, only I was going get them harder.

I am a very passionate person. I love so hard; I might love too hard at times, but when I do something for people, it really is out the kindness of my heart, so when I'm in a situation and I need somebody to help me or somebody isn't taking the initiative to help me, it really bothers because I go out of my way so often for people just to make them happy with the little things.

I was in the sixth grade when I ran back into Briana Spragens. We had recently gotten a call from Webster over that little boy Sebastian. I definitely got over him real fast, but that's how Briana and I became close friends. Briana's mom, my godmother Shon, was very involved in her school life. Shon was coming to the school every day or every other day popping in on Bri and making sure nobody was messing with her. When I was one of the kids who was messing with her, Shon approached me instead of telling me to go get my mama. She became a mother to me. Briana was nonchalant about a lot of stuff, and it was easy to tell that she was spoiled. A lot of girls didn't like her basically because she had a big ass booty. One time, we had to have partners and chaperones for a field trip, and Shon was one of those volunteers. I was in Briana's group, and I remember Shon and I were kicking it off. At this time, Briana and I weren't that close, but we were getting closer. I think Briana had already told her mom that I was kind of a bully, so I think Shon had to fill me out to see if I really was one. Later on, she figured out I had the same trauma as she did as a child with my parents suffering from substance abuse.

THE STRUGGLE THAT MADE ME

Even though Elmhurst was on 98th,' the school itself was cool if you wanted it to be. Mistah F.A.B. came to Elmhurst to talk to the students about his life. He spoke very well, and it was really touching to hear him touch on the things he'd been going through and how he overcame his struggles from the beginning to the end. At this time, he'd just put out his new song that became local platinum. Mistah F.A.B. contributed a lot to the hyphy movement even though it was already established, but he was definitely coming up at that time. He expressed his love for music and told us about his child who overcame a lot of obstacles. I remember feeling empathy and touched by his story and admired how he wanted more out of life. At the school, we also had sewing classes and other projects where we had to take care of a baby. It cried all the time, and I damn near wanted to throw that baby out the window. I even learned how to play the flute at ECP. Even though I was dealing with a lot of stuff, I still took advantage of things that interested me just to get my mind off of home. I was very creative, and I loved to do things with my imagination. Because I was in middle school, there were a lot of people dressing up and looking nice, and I felt dirty. I knew I was less fortunate, so I tried my hardest to keep myself up, however I had to get a summer job because I was so tired of asking my mom for five or ten dollars. She sometimes had to ask other people to give the money to me. Major was making a few dollars, but I knew what he was going through, so I tried not to ask him for anything. He always made sure I ate, and if I really needed something, he would buy if for me.

After school one time, I saw a flyer nailed to a tree advertising work for teens. When I called the number, a man named Bill answered the phone. He told me if I wanted to work that I had to be serious and that I could make some really good money. I was so ready to start doing stuff for myself. I was so tired of looking how I did. He told me to be ready the next day to work, even though I didn't know exactly what I was going to be doing. The next day, he picked me up from school after talking with my mom. Mama approved of me going even though she was very skeptical and didn't want me around any men without her supervision. But Bill was hella cool, and I never got a bad feeling from him. The first week I worked for Bill, he picked up about seven to ten kids every day, and we went around San Leandro and Oakland selling items. We sold good products like turtles and cover mugs. We even went as far as Bakersfield on the weekends when we didn't have school. Working for Bill is how I met another boy named Santiago. He was Sandy's brother, who was in my class at Webster. Santiago and I were some of Bill's best salespeople, and we'd have competitions where whoever sold the most items would get 200 extra dollars. I was so determined to win that 200 bucks. Santiago was handsome, and he knew how to persuade people very well. I, on the other hand, learned how to speak well but was a dirty little girl, so Santiago won most of our competitions. But I was pretty close behind him a lot of time, and Bill was very satisfied with what I was bringing in. One time, I was so determined to win the 200 dollars that I wouldn't leave every house or gas station or store until I got a donation or a contribution for the Teen Leaders of California.

My daddy taught me how to box at a young age. He used to put up both of his hands and let me punch, saying, "One, one, two, one, one, two, upper cut, right hook, left hook, duck. You gotta learn how to keep your guards up, Kiki!" I loved to fight not because I like to hurt people but because I love the technique of fighting. Also my brother beat my ass, so I was determined to learn how to fight. I was never scared of any women ever in my life. It was a dream to be stronger and faster than my big brother, which never happened, but in my head, I wanted to be stronger and smarter than him. Knowing how to fight help me feel confident while working because I was ready to protect myself if someone ever thought about snatching me up.

I won the bonus! I was so excited that I was making my own little money. I could buy myself lunch and snacks from the snack bar at Elmhurst. They had these hot chips with cheese that were amazing.

I got to know Briana a lot more when the whole class went camping and had an outdoor experience. We became really close on that field trip, and I started spending the night over at her house. Her mom, Shon, treated me like her own kid. When she bought Briana an outfit, she bought me one, too. If I was hungry, she bought me something to eat or taught Briana and I how to cook and clean the kitchen. Shaneta was a fine, young mama. She had three kids at this point, but now that mama has about ten. I'm putting it on a little thick, but she has a lot of kids.

Briana and I did everything together—we went to school together, studied together, even fucked with her little brother Melvin together. We made Melvin's life a living hell. He hated when I came over. One time we waited until

Melvin went to sleep, and then we put some playboy ice cubes all over him, and whenever he would move or we thought he was going to wake up, we would run to the closet. It took about five times for him to catch on to what we were doing, and when he finally found out it was us, he screamed out, "Kasandra, Briana, I hate you! Get out of my room!" I think the only reason he woke up is because we could not stop laughing.

I loved going over Briana's house even though she was spoiled, and that made me feel less than her at times. She sometimes made me want to beat her ass, but I didn't because I loved her so much. She was one of the girls that I couldn't hurt. Shaneta didn't know that my mom was on drugs until I told her, and it took me a while to get to that point. I had already told Briana about what was going on with me, and that's why she wanted me to come over her house all the time. It was so good to confide in Shaneta because my godmom had been through the same things as me. She told me her mom was also on drugs and was an addict ever since she was young. She expressed to me that she went through a lot of hardship due to her mom's substance abuse, but she did not let that define her. She never let anything define her, not even the fact she was about twenty-four with three kids.

I loved to tell Briana and her mom stories because I always had them cracking up and on their backs. Even I was on my back laughing at the shit I used to say and think about. One thing about Mama Shon, though, is she did not play that shit with Briana's ass. One day, Briana and I were playing in the house, and Briana thought it would be a great idea to hide in her mom's dryer downstairs. That bitch thought she had a great hiding spot, and it was because I couldn't find her. I thought she went outside somewhere. Finally, I went downstairs to use the bathroom, and as I was on the toilet, I thought I heard somebody laughing hella hard. I opened up the door to see her mom was whipping Briana all the way from the dryer to the upstairs room. She was beating Briana so bad, Briana's cries sounded like laughter. I bet that bitch regretted hiding in the dryer because of that ass whipping. After that, Briana didn't want to talk to me. She was so mad because she thought I let her mama come down there on purpose, but if I'd known Briana was in the dryer, I would've told her not to hide there because her mama paid a lot of money for it. That was the first time I saw Briana get a good ass whooping, and I didn't want to come out the bathroom because I thought Mama Shon was going to whip my ass, too, but in a soft voice, she said, "Kasandra, I'm not mad at you, baby. I'm mad at Briana. Don't think that you're getting in trouble, too, because your ass wasn't the one in the dryer."

Chapter 7

When we moved to Walnut from Sunnyside, my cousins started to come over less often. At this time, I was really close to one of my second cousins on my dad's side. I really looked up to her. She was so pretty, light-skinned, petite, and thick with beautiful eyes and a decent grade of hair. She had another little sister who was a straight crybaby and a snitch. I think she was a little slower at learning than my other cousins because she would still drool on herself a little bit, and I remember my dad had to change her at like four years old because she'd shitted herself. My dad had to do it because my mom couldn't take the smell. She had a very weak stomach. My cousin's mom was selling dope at the time, so my cousin was really the only one coming over on Walnut because she needed a place to be. All my other cousins still came when we had our parties or little gatherings, but for the most part my cousin on my dad's side came way more often. I got really close to her because her mom would always drop her and her sister off. My second cousin and I would choreograph dances, write songs, and play fight. One time we went with my dad to the creek at Dimond Park, and we crawled all the way from the beginning to the end of the tunnel. Even though I was scared, my dad pushed me to go with him. It was very adventurous. My cousin was very athletic as well, and we competed in a lot of things. We even competed with my brothers. I remember one time she beat Major at the park, and he was hella mad. My cousin had a beautiful spirit even though she had anxiety issues and she didn't like certain noises. I didn't really notice that my cousin was kind of off, however. Even though she was really smart in school and had her little boyfriend, certain things would really irritate her, and I didn't understand why until later on.

My cousin was the one who introduced me to sex. I knew a little about it, but my cousin broke it down for me by describing how a baby is actually made—the penis in the coochie, all of that. She was a couple years older than me, so she was more advanced and experienced having had puppy love with her boyfriend at the time. They later had two kids together. I will talk a lot about that in my second book. My cousin was way more advanced than me. I could tell she was doing shit she wasn't supposed to be doing. Once, we even gave each other hickeys. She told me to give her one, and my dumbass gave her a hickey right on her cheek. We tried to put a spoon on it to take the color away, but the hickey was so big and she was so light-skinned that it showed regardless. I wound up getting in trouble with my mom for doing that even though my cousin had asked me to. I was never attracted to girls, however my cousin was. I remember she told me to get under the bed so nobody could see us, and she kissed me on my mouth. From that point on, I knew I wasn't into women. Each time she would go further and further, and it made me wonder where knew how to do all these sexual things. I didn't realize she was molesting me. I got out from under the bed, wiped my mouth, and told her I didn't like that. She never tried anything like that again, and she apologized about it later on.

My cousin loved coming over to my house, and I didn't understand why all my cousins loved my house so much. I asked her if I could spend the night over at her house one time, and she was really hesitant to say yes. I could tell she wanted me to spend the night but at the same time she didn't for some reason. I told her that I didn't want to be at my house and that I wanted to go over to hers and play. She asked her mom if I could spend the night, and she said yes. At the time, her mom was dating a man with a lot of girls and boys. His kids were about five to ten years older than me and Briana. I remember going over my cousin's house for a whole summer because I didn't want to stay home. My cousin was so happy that I spent a whole summer with her. During that summer, we went to waterparks and movies in the park. We met up with little boys and tried to be flirty. I was still a virgin, so I wasn't thinking about sex; I just wanted to spend some time with a boy. One time we got caught by my cousin's friend. She saw us talking to some guys at the park, and she told on us. We didn't get a whooping or anything, but we definitely got yelled at.

One time while I was staying the night over at my cousin's house, I told my cousin's stepsister that I liked it this boy named Kevin, who went to Elmhurst with me. I told her that Kevin and I kissed, and I wanted to have sex with him. Though Briana had explained what sex is, I didn't really understand it at this point. I just knew I liked Kevin, and I wanted him to like me, too. My cousin's stepsister told my auntie, and I got a whooping. My cousin's mom thought I was fast because I was fighting and running the streets. She didn't know I was still a virgin. Little did she know her own daughter already had practiced sexual acts on me.

THE STRUGGLE THAT MADE ME

My auntie also didn't know her daughter was getting raped by her boyfriend at the time. From age five to fourteen, my cousin was assaulted with a big ass dick in a little girl's private part. My cousin confided in me he was raping her when I told her about the weird behavior her stepdad was exhibiting toward me. The first incident happened when we went to Raging Waters waterpark. He was dipping me up and down in the water, and I felt his dick on my butt getting harder and harder. I thought I was tripping, so I didn't say anything, but I was kind of shaken by it. The second incident took place when I was putting on my bathing suit to go swimming with my cousin. He came in the bathroom while I was completely naked, looked me up and down for about eight seconds, and then closed the door. I was in shock. I didn't really know what to do. I thought maybe he'd done it on accident because I've never experienced anything like this with my father. He never touched me or made me feel like he was trying to molest me, so I gave my cousin's stepfather the benefit of the doubt. It wasn't until my auntie went to work to sell drugs that I realized he was a pedophile. It was like he waited until she left to ask me to give him a good morning kiss but I knew that I wasn't supposed to be kissing a grown man.

My mama instilled in me from when I was young to never kiss men on the cheek and to never be alone with them. My mom was very serious about teaching me this due to her past and her upbringing at the church home. When he asked me for a kiss, I knew something was wrong. I knew I shouldn't have been giving him a kiss because he wouldn't have asked me for that if my big cousin or auntie had been around, but I leaned in to kiss him on the cheek, and he turned my face to try to stick his tongue down my throat. It was like he was waiting to do that for a long time. It felt like he was infatuated with me—my face and my body. Whenever nobody was looking, I would catch him staring at me with his face all red like he wanted to eat me alive. After he tried to kiss me, I ran in the room to Briana. I was in shock. I told her what happened, and that's when her eyes lit up. She started tearing up, and she sat me down. That's when she told me he had been raping her since she was five. We cried and we cried and we cried. She revealed all of it to me. She even told me his sons were raping her, too. I felt so bad for my cousin, I wanted to kill everybody who hurt her. Why would anyone traumatize a young girl like that? She explained to me that she was fucked in the ass and had to swallow his cum. She had to take big ass dick since she was hella little. That man took her virginity at five years old.

45

Why she was so sexual and why she was so confused about her worth and how much she actually meant as a young lady suddenly made sense to me. I didn't know how she could go on that long without telling her mom. I asked her if she tried to talk to my auntie, and she said that she hadn't explicitly told her, but she'd given her mom so many signs to where any mother should have known. I felt like my auntie knew her daughter was getting raped. My older cousin had mentioned the man touching her, but nobody believed her because she was a little older in everybody thought she was fast. I told Briana I was going to tell my mom and my dad, and my brother was going to kill him, but Briana begged me not to say anything. Instead, she asked me to tell her mom that her stepdad tried to kiss me. When she came back from selling dope, Briana called her mom into the room, and I could tell she knew something was wrong. I told her that her husband tried to kiss me on the mouth, and I also told her about his coming into the bathroom to seeing me naked. My auntie acted like she was so mad. She said she was going to have a long talk with him and that it would never happen again, but she asked me to never tell my family because it would make everyone turn against her, and she didn't want my mom to fight with her.

She dropped me off at home a couple of days later, but she came into my mom's house to distract me, so I couldn't say anything. She wanted to be sure that I'd forgotten what her husband did to me. I put it in the back of my head, but I couldn't stop thinking about my cousin and how I was the only person who knew what was going on. I felt like I needed to keep her secret until she was strong enough to come out on her own. That was the last time I ever went over to her house because I was so scared I was going to get raped.

When my cousin was fourteen, she finally told an adult her stepdad was raping her. She said he had fucked the shit out of her, and that was the last time she could take it. She ran to the fire station, broke down crying, and told the firefighters the man been raping her ever since she was five years old. I was so relieved that my cousin told the truth. I was so happy he wasn't ever going to rape her again. She told everyone everything from how her stepdad was raping her to how his sons were raping her, too. She even told the therapist the man was raping his own daughters. What type of sick fuck rapes his own daughters? That's just nasty as fuck, and that was the same daughter who told on me about wanting to have sex with Kevin. Like girl, your daddy was fucking you, and you're going to tell on *me* about trying to have sex?

THE STRUGGLE THAT MADE ME

My cousin's mom made her boyfriend flee. He should have gone to jail forever, but Briana's mom made her lie and say that it didn't happen, so the case was closed. Briana had a real boyfriend at the time, and the thought of her getting fucked by her stepdad while having a boyfriend was crazy to me. She couldn't even love who she wanted to love. Briana later had kid with that boyfriend and got the kids to do to her mental state by being raped damn near all her young life. She was on crystal meth and all kinds of other drugs later on in life, and this is why I am writing this book. Shit like this has to stop. I wasn't the one getting raped, but I feel like I was. That's how much I love my family. When they tell me something, I feel their pain, and Briana's situation was really eating at me because I couldn't tell anybody until she was ready to share the truth. She showed me marks from cutting herself and said if I told anyone what was happening she'd kill herself. But she'd been wanted to kill herself for a long time. She tried attempting so many times, but nothing quite worked. I honestly didn't know how her mom didn't see all the marks on her thighs, legs, and her stomach. I beat myself up about that all the time because I feel like her life might have played out differently if I had spoken up sooner, but I can't think that way because I was just a child. The adults needed to be accountable for their actions.

My cousin's mom wound up isolating herself from the family. I guess she was ashamed, or she didn't want to talk about how she was with men who wanted her kids or how she wanted to make men happy more than her children. Briana even told me that she saved her sister from getting raped by telling one of the brothers to take her instead. I thought to myself, why would anybody want a shitty booty ass little girl, but you know those boys were sick at the time. I guess they'd worn my cousin's pussy out so much that they wanted her little sister.

One day, I was called out of school and taken to a place where Child Protective Services talks to kids. I remember walking into the room and seeing my mom crying. She told me she loved me and asked if I was raped by my cousin's stepdad, too. I told her he did not rape me, but I was honest about what he did to me at Raging Waters, how he watched me naked, and how he kissed me. My mom was very pissed off, and I don't think my dad could even come to CPS because he was so mad and he didn't know what to do or say. I don't know if he was mad at my cousin or not, but he wasn't at the meeting. Eventually, this lady came in and told me she was a counselor and I needed to be honest about everything I knew about my cousin. I told her I was so happy to tell someone finally, so my cousin would stop getting raped. It was like a huge weight was lifted off my shoulders. My brother, on the other hand, did not take it very well when he found out. He exploded. He wanted to kill everybody and everything. He felt much better knowing I hadn't been raped, but he still was mad that I'd experienced gross behavior.

At this point, Major was in and out of my life because he wanted to move with my Uncle Boo to the Discovery Bay/Pittsburgh area for a better life. My mom wasn't happy about that even though Major was going to do it anyway because he was fed up being around all of the drug abuse. He was tired of being our father figure. He wanted to get away and have more freedom. I think it was a good decision for him even though he still got caught up in some bad stuff later on, but it wasn't until he came back to live with us in West Oakland that he received his first attempted murder charge.

Chapter 8

When we were still living on Walnut, Mexicans lived next door to us. Maria, the mom, enjoyed that my mom would always borrow money from across the street. She had twins, Mikey and Kamari, and Ray Ray, Keshad, and I loved going over there to play. I would also play with some girls down the street, and we make dances and play flight. I was the only girl, so I always had to find some girls to play with, but I didn't get along with a lot of the girls I met.

Our landlord was black, and I remember her two boys. I think his name was Killum, but I forgot the little boy's name. They were kind of nervous and had some money. She owned the building we were renting on section eight, and for the most part, our landlord was cool, but I remember my mom saying little things here and there about how she didn't like us doing certain things. Some were not that big of a deal, but others I could understand. One time, my brother and I found some sort of spray can bottle, and we wrote "90 Sunnyside" on the whole side of the fence. We'd just moved from Sunnyside, and I wanted to represent it everywhere I went, but I didn't know my mama had to pay for that shit, and we paid with an ass whooping. Not to mention we spelled Sunnyside wrong.

I was still going to Elmhurst at that time, and my behavior was getting worse and worse due to what I was going through at home. I mean, I really used to take out my anger on people. Some might've deserved it, but others didn't deserve it at all. One time, I brought a knife to school to scare people, and another time I was messing with this Latina girl by constantly kicking her chair. She was so irritated, she turned around and told me she'd give me twenty dollars if I stopped. After school, I walked with her all the way to the E Morris docks where her mom didn't speak no English and her little brother was at school picking them up. I really thought this girl owed me twenty dollars, like my stupid ass really followed this girl, and she knew I had a knife. If I were her, I would've been whipping my ass. I don't know what made me think I was entitled to her money, but I guess it was because she had promised she'd give it to me. One of the other students said I was chasing the girl and told the principal on me. I got the DHP from school the next day. I remember because it was a Friday, and we had our townhall meeting. The students would sing this song, E C P that stated with "I love my gray and black. Nothing how hold us back." The whole school used to be turned up off of that chant. The boy I had a crush on, Kevin, used to start the whole song off, by beating on the table like it was a drum, that shit used to not be knocking, but we used to start singing it anyway.

At the time I was a 4.0 student. I literally had all A's. I was very smart, and I challenged myself to be smarter and smarter. I even remember winning a metaphor and simile essay over an Indian girl. I was very intellectual, and nobody really understood me. They just thought I was troublesome, but they knew I was very smart.

A few of my family members came to stay with us when we moved to Walnut. I remember my Uncle Rashad, my cousin Ros Lamb, my cousin Delano, and even my granny before she moved to Acorn High-Rises. She lived with us until my mom put her out. Uncle Rashad was my dad's little brother. They were about thirteen years apart, so he was really young. He's a Sunnyside original, like really original. He hung out there with his two best friends, and I call them my uncles as well to this day. They're still all really tight. My uncle wasn't a hard ass or a killer, but he was a hustler getting money and selling. He lived his best life on Sunnyside. My uncle didn't have too many problems with people. He was really solid and not into bullshit. I guess that's how he and his friends ended up living this long, the three amigos. I'm sure they've seen a lot of people come and go, and it's only by the grace of God they're still living. I can't imagine the shit they faced on Sunnyside, but I remember my uncle staying with us for a minute. I think he was married around that time. My uncle loved dirt bikes. I remember he let us ride one of them. He put me on a bike, and I tried to takeoff immediately. He grabbed my body and let the bike run into the fence. He started cracking up like, "Oh Poodie! You would've been done!"

My uncle did not have a close relationship with me until I got older. He had a closer relationship with my other first cousins, including my auntie's daughter, the one who was killed by Booker while trying to help her friend. I understood why my uncle was closer to my cousins. My cousin Vlonne was only eight when she lost my auntie, and my other cousin was only nine months old. I looked up to both of my cousins. They didn't have the same dad, so one of my cousins stayed with her dad, John Nisha, who went to New Mexico, and my other cousin, Vlonne, basically moved in with my granny and her new husband Billy after they moved from us. My cousin was in a relationship with this boy named Reggie, and they were in puppy love. They lied and left her some for Reggie. Reggie left her alone, but Reggie hit licks and went straight to Lana every time. I loved the bond that they had, and they were really nasty, too. I remember going everywhere with my cousin Delana because she was forced to take me. She was so mad she had to take me everywhere. Reggie stayed on 73rd, and I loved going over to his house because I got to go see my friend Lila. She had a lot of brothers and sisters from the Mabons, and we all went to school together.

Lana and Reggie fell apart after Reggie kept cheating on her with a bitch named Slick Bag. My cousin caught that bitch because she said she'll go straight to jail, straight back. I later asked my cousin why she and Reggie didn't work out because I really wanted them to have a baby together, but my cousin explained that Slick Bag was the type of bitch that did anything for him, and Lana wasn't about to do *everything* for him. I mean, she would help Reggie but wasn't ready to take care of him like that. I guess he wanted somebody to always be around.

After Delana moved out, it was back to just Ray Ray, Keshad, Major, and me. Greg was away with his girlfriend at this time being Moe. My brother called himself this when he was trying to be a fake pimp. That kid a pimp! But he was in love. Back at the house on Walnut, we had new neighbors move in next door. They were a single mother, her two sons, and her daughter named Neicy. Neicy always wore two French braids. I mean, every time I saw her she had those two French braids. Major was really cool with the neighbor's sons, and I think he even liked the daughter, too. We would play basketball and tag outside, and we'd visit the neighbors upstairs until the little boy cried and I'd have to go home.

I'd often visit the Mexicans' house next door. They always had food over there, and they always threw parties. They loved for us to come visit, and they were always very generous, but the Mexican kids were really bad. This little boy named Angel would fuck up his brother Fernando. He reminded me of a little Chucky. Everybody in the house treated Angel like he was a baby, and that only made it worse. He used to curse in every sentence. I noticed that a lot of Mexican Americans got away with that when they were young because their parents didn't know which words were bad or not in English. I remember Angel used to be like "Fuck you bitch!" to his mama, and his mama would just say,

"Angel, no don't say that." Most kids didn't get away with things like that. He did whatever he wanted to do just like little Stewie in "Family Guy."

My brothers and I always used to play outside, and one day we were riding these big ass bikes, and my little brother Ray Ray wanted to show me that he could ride the bike with no hands, and as he was trying, he wound up falling hella hard. I remember the bike rolling slowly when he took his hands off the handlebars, and the bike slowed down to a complete stop and my brother went down with it. I guess he thought the bike was still going to roll, but he cried. He was so hurt. I also remember us having a party. I forgot whose birthday it was, but I remember all of my cousins coming over, and that's when this song came on: "I'm a tell your daddy; tell my daddy. I'm a call your daddy; call my daddy. You so mad; I'm so mad. You just mad cause you ain't my daddy..." (Hitman Sammy Sam, 2003).

At this point, my daddy was twirling a bill in a circular motion with his eyes closed in a game where we all tried not to get swatted by the bill. We played this outside for a whole hour. My dad was hella drunk, and we had hella fun. It was so fun trying not to get whipped by the bill even though my daddy really whipped us in real life with a belt. But still it was fun.

Chapter 9

At this point, Major was coming home less than less. He was staying away from my dad and my mom, but he would come over on the weekends. One time, we walked into the store to get some candy, and when we came back to our street corner, the neighbor's dog was loose. It was hella big. It looked like a Labrador mixed with something else, and I remember freezing up because I'd never seen a dog outside like that. I could tell my brother was scared, too, but knowing that I was terrified and the dog was about to attack, Major stepped in front of me and used his brown paper bag that we'd got from the store to scare the dog off. My brother really stood up for me in that moment. He was ready to get attacked by the dog over his little sister, but luckily the owner came out just in time and told the dog to go back inside. That was one of the instances I felt protected by my brother. Even though he often picked on me and teased me, he always came through when I needed him to, and I really appreciated that.

Major at the time used to go to the barbershop around the corner from our house on E. 14th right next to Moses music. He looked up this man named Marty, who we both considered an uncle. Marty kept Major out of trouble and also kept a couple of dollars in his pocket, Marty had a nephew named Chris Tha Fifth, who put out an album, and when I say we played that album from song one to sixteen, I mean we played it all the time. I still know the songs. I love all of them, but the one that I really loved went like this:

"If I had another chance, I do things a little different. Got everything I need, but it's you that I'm missing when it comes to my attention that all these hoes I'm getting a were nothing because I rather you girl. I am digging you, and I know you want me too, but it seems like all these calls I get are never coming through, but it's cool 'cause I got a couple bitches coming through, but it ain't worth it because I rather be with you" (Chris Tha Fifth, 2004).

That album should have gone platinum on all platforms. It was the early 2000s, so people didn't have YouTube or anything like that back then, but Chris Tha Fifth is definitely a legend in my book. He is one of the reasons why I started writing and rapping. He had a vision when he rapped. I can picture the shit he was saying and how he felt when he wrote everything, and obviously

Major did, too. Major used to get in his feelings a lot and play music. When he was missing my Auntie Stephanie, he played "I'll Be Missing You" on repeat.

I loved how my brother expressed himself and had all his feelings, and even though Major wasn't my dad's real child, my dad's side of the family accepted him as family. He and Delana were especially close back at the house, but that wasn't enough. One night when we were getting ready to move to 61st, Major came in the house high. I think my dad was drunk and mad because he couldn't get any more crack from the dope man who used to deal to my parents. I knew this because when my parents used to get high, I would listen to every conversation they had. I knew when they were smoking because it had started to become a routine. At the time, I remember my dad pinning my brother up against the wall outside. I saw in my brother's eyes that he was so fed up. He was the type who didn't like to cry, but when he cried, I could feel how hurt he was. I hated it when my brother cried because anytime he did, I felt so bad. I hated it when he wanted to run away or he would tell us that he wasn't ever coming back. That shit hurt me because I needed my brother. I needed my father figure. I needed my protector. I don't blame him for doing what he had to do, but he really put me in a situation where my father's anger was taken out on my other brothers and me because Major was gone. My daddy whooped my little brother Keshad, but it wouldn't be like ours because he was light-skinned, and my mom always told my daddy to not put any marks on him because he bruised easily. There were times that my dad would whoop our asses because we couldn't find the smallest shit. Sometimes he would have to remind us for a few days, but with my parents being on drugs, some days they didn't give a fuck and some days they did. The days that they did were the days we got her asses whooped. But when they were on drugs and we fucked up their high, we really got her asses whooped, so it was like damned if we do, damned if we don't.

One time, my daddy was chasing my little brother Ray Ray because he couldn't remember something my dad had asked him. I just remember my dad having a belt in his hand, my dad asked about whatever he had done for that to happen, and I could tell Ray Ray's mind was blank. He shouted to my daddy that his mind wasn't working. He was so serious, and I knew exactly what my brother was talking about because when somebody yelled at me, I'd try to comprehend what they were saying, but I couldn't because I knew I was about to get my ass whooped. Fortunately, right after Ray Ray said that, my daddy couldn't even whip his ass because he started busting out laughing. My dad thought the fact that he couldn't think was so funny, but if Ray Ray hadn't said that, his ass would've gotten a good beating. I remember that day because I had just fed our goldfish, the red devil and Oscar, in the nice sized tank.

Ray Ray was doing an excellent job now that he was going to Encompass Academy. He was very in tune with school, and he really wanted to learn more and more every day. He loved what he learned in school, and he appreciated that the school had a way of teaching kids how to analyze things on a different level. I love that for him because Ray Ray had really been going down the wrong path. Miss Maisie really saved my brother's mental state and gave him the opportunity to learn a lot more than he could at Webster. Webster wasn't a bad school, but it definitely wasn't the right school for my little brother to excel and learn and do better.

Webster had typing class and an afterschool tennis program that I loved to go to. Tennis was actually the first sport I was interested in other than tee-ball, which my brother and I played at Brookfield. We were the best at tee-ball. Playing in the peewee league was the only time Ray Ray and I actually played a sport together. My dad didn't have a car at the time, so we had to hitch rides and ask people to take us places, but the coaches and other parents did not mind picking us up because we were the heart of the team. We were always really motivated and worked hard to become winners. I remember taking our team picture when we got our jerseys. It felt really good to get a jersey and feel a part of something with my little brother, so I felt like I had to be better than everybody else. I think I was the only girl on the team. The coaches were so happy to have us on their team, and they had me on first base every time because I wouldn't ever give the other team a chance. Sometimes I would even run to the outfield and still strike them out. I would run and catch the ball and quickly strike them out.

My dad pushed us to be the best at sports, so that's part of the reason I was so competitive. I mean, I was always competing with my big brother or younger brother, so I was ready to win everything, and I gave it my all every time after school in tennis. We used to all pile into a big van and go to UC Berkeley where we'd practice. I remember one instructor's name was Nick, and the other instructor was our computer teacher at Webster, Ms. Tiffany. Miss

Tiffany thought she was the shit, and I'm not just saying that. This lady played tennis in heels! Shit, I guess she was the shit playing tennis in heels.

The first time I ever saw somebody have a seizure was at Bear Tracks, our tennis program. This boy named Charles also had a little brother, and he was one of the people in the tennis after school program. We'd have to run laps before we started playing tennis, and I remember Charles all of the sudden fall to the ground on the court and foaming at the mouth. Mr. Nick was so scared, he turned pink. I was kind of in shock because I didn't know what was going on with him. Miss Tiffany immediately told everybody to go to the portables, and all I remember is the ambulance showing up and Charles looking like he was about to die. Eventually he came back to school, and I was so happy to see that he was okay.

I also remember the security guard at Webster whose name was Valerie. She was hella cool, but when the bell started ringing, we had to get our asses in class. I liked to be on good terms with Valerie, and I wanted to make sure she didn't lose her job or have to whip my ass outside of school. She had a couple nieces and nephews who went to Webster, and she made sure nobody touched them back on Walnut.

At this point, Major was going back and forth between home and Discovery Bay. He would come home every now and then to make sure his little brothers and sister were okay, but for the most part, Major was gone. He never wanted to be home. My little brother Keshad is like Major in a lot of ways. Major always got into it. One time, he came home from Sunnyside or from wherever he was, and Major was feeling some type away about the fact my mom never circumcised any of her boys when they were babies. Major actually wound up getting the procedure to get the extra skin taken off. He was walking around with a limp and talking a lot of shit to me, telling me where he was going and how he needed me to clean up more than him. I was already fed up with his ass, and I was tired of fighting him. I knew that he was in one of his weakest moments, so I started talking shit, which made him walk up to me, and as soon as he did, I kicked him right in his dick. He was in the most excruciating pain I've ever seen him in at that moment. There's not a whipping my daddy could've given him to feel that type of pain. He couldn't even talk. He couldn't do anything. I felt really bad afterward, but at the same time, I had to get him good. He'd tortured me my whole life, and I wanted to make a statement that day.

I was tired of getting slapped around. I didn't want to get my ass whooped because I was strong. My daddy taught Major and me how to box, but my daddy focused on me more because Major was recognizing how much stronger and faster I was getting. But that didn't stop him from teasing me and calling me all types of names, so I started roasting his ass back. I wasn't about to let him keep talking to me like crazy. I hated it when he'd talked about my daddy and how he wasn't shit, but at the same time, everything he said was true. I'd reply that at least I had a daddy, which was really fucked up because my brother's dad was not in his life at all. In fact, Major's name is another man's name. Major Session was a man my mother was with when she was pregnant with Major, but Major's real dad's name is Winston. I could imagine all of the pain my brother went through, not knowing his biological father, and it didn't help that my dad was constantly drunk and trying to chastise him. Despite all of that, however, my dad was the closest thing to a father he would ever have, and I'm sure my brother would love him for everything. He taught him good and bad because I love my dad regardless of how much he whipped our asses or how much he didn't understand. I love my daddy so much, and I really thank him for teaching me how to be strong. But the time I kicked Major in the groin was the last time he fucked with me just to be fucking with me. We did have mini fights later on as we got older, but it wasn't about dumb shit anymore. As we aged, we really grew to hate each other, but at the same time we're so happy when we get to see each other. We're both Virgos, so we clashed over everything, but I can't honestly say my brother really shaped me into becoming a protector and a provider. All I did was mimic his actions wherever he was.

We did have some great father figures in our life. my mom made this man named Fred my goddaddy, and I know why now. He was The Godfather of 1990s at Sunnyside. He was sharp and always stayed fresh and had a good outfit with style. When we lived on Sunnyside, he always made sure we had a couple of dollars in our pocket. He never looked at my mom in any type of way because he knew how good her heart was, and he trusted the light of our blessings would shine because of how good hearted she was. People loved my mom so much for that, even though there were some people that talked down on her at her lowest moments, but she was always okay because my mama was born into this world lonely and already heartbroken. She chose to have her kids despite her struggles, and we were never taken by the system even though we could have been, but I always tell her that just because she was functional doesn't make it right. It doesn't mean I don't have trauma. Just because we weren't homeless and hungry doesn't mean everything was perfect.

Chapter 10

The landlord on Walnut also owned an inflatable jumper company, and I loved that because every time they had a party, they had big jumpers, and we had so much fun. A lot of people stayed with us on Walnut as well. There were a lot of people coming in and out, having to sleep on our couch for weeks or months, giving my mama nothing or a couple dollars here and there, talking about her but needing her at the same time. I remember there was this couple that lived with us, and my mom was so sweet and nice to them. They were both suffering from drug addiction, but eventually my mama got too comfortable around the couple and kept leaving money around, and they wound up stealing about 500 dollars from my mom. A lot of people stole from my mom, everyone from cousins to friends, but my mom always made a way for us to live, and we were blessed, not always in the way we wanted but always when we needed to be. I'm sure those people will pay for their actions later because God watches everything. I knew he was watching, so I started trying to be better even though I knew my mom was smoking and I was dealing with a lot just being a young girl. I also recall one of my older cousins who I call my uncle cooking crack. Well, we had to go in the room. I remember because I could smell it. my mom would tell us when to come out the room but even when we came out it was a very distinctive smell. I know he would give my mom crack in order to cook up his dope. This put us in Jeopardy not only by CPS but by other people that might have wanted to rob our house. I had thought to myself, *Why is everyone usin' our house for their dirt? Why can't they go over their own house?*

My mama took care of us to the extent where she definitely made sure we had a roof over our heads and the little hand-me-downs on our backs. She tried her best, allowing us to enjoy different sports and participate in athletics as much as we could. My dad was very athletic, so he pushed us very hard to be the best. He even put Major in sports. Unfortunately they didn't have enough money for everything, like when I wanted to join the Oakland Dynamites cheer team. I wanted to be a Dynamite so badly, and I even sat and watched their practice at 96 Sunnyside Park all the time. I even joined when they had practice sometimes, and I learned how to do all types of things, but I was so sad because I knew that I wasn't going to be able to tour with them. They also wanted me on their team because I was just that good. I knew how to do the splits and starts the dances. I have really good balance, and I was really strong.

I was, however, able to join the karate class at Arroyo Viejo with Ray Ray. We loved to learn different techniques of fighting. We also played the Nintendo, but our Nintendo was so old, we had to blow into the chips to make them work. We love playing Mortal Kombat and looking at different fighting styles, trying to anticipate each other by using different moves that we learned from Major. One time I was working with this boy in the karate class and I wasn't supposed to give it my all, but I did not understand the difference between fighting and practicing then. I just remember us touching gloves and my kicking him straight in the head like Jackie Chan. In fact, he would've been impressed because of how impactful my kick was. The instructor immediately stopped the fight, and I was on a time out afterward. While I was sitting out, he walked up to me, put his hand on my shoulder, and told me he wasn't mad and I had a gift. He told me to keep going, but I had to get out the class because my mom didn't have enough money. It was a free trial for only one month, but I was glad we had that experience because I really wanted to join a karate class.

Major was always in my business whenever he came back around. I don't know if he wanted to know if I was doing stuff I wasn't supposed to in terms of having sex and dealing with boys, but I definitely wasn't going through anything like that around this time. I mean, I liked the boys, but I wasn't having sex or being extra fast like people thought for whatever reason. I was just fighting and trying to smoke weed here and there. It wasn't until about sixth or seventh grade that I really went on my first date with this boy named Charles. Charles went to EZ Pay with me, and he was so charming to me. He was kind of light-skinned, had a cute smell, and was so sweet, but he was a little boy, and that really made me like him even more. He wasn't super bad, but he was a little bad. I remember he asked me to go to the carnival with him, and I was so excited because it was the first time a boy actually had the balls to ask me on an actual date. I felt so special. I couldn't wait to go to the carnival with Charles, so I made sure I hustled up enough money that week with Bill to get myself something cute for the date. I was so scared to tell my mommy he asked me out, but she was actually happy for me, and she wanted me to go with us to the carnival.

I remember when Charles picked me up from my house on 61st and Avanal street, and his mom was so pretty. She was hella young compared to my mom, and she was very sweet, so I could tell she liked me even though I was less fortunate. When we went to the carnival, his mom let us wander around laughing until shit started getting too funny. We got on a ride where we had to stand on the wall while the machine spun around. We were stuck to the wall spinning in circles when Charles started acting like he was all big and bad. He tried to hold onto the rail while we were on the ride, but as it got faster and faster, he couldn't help but release his hand, and he smacked me right in my eye. That's the first time I'd ever seen real stars. He felt so bad and was so embarrassed that he was trying to be mister macho, so I was walking around that motherfucker with a blackeye laughing and smiling after he gave a cute teddy bear. I was hella mad he hit me, though, but I knew he didn't do it on purpose.

The next ride we got on was the Big Zipper and, I don't really know if he threw up, but I know it wasn't me. Fortunately as we got on the ride, we shared a kiss, and it was the cutest thing to me, but as we got off there was throw up all over us. He swore up and down that he didn't do it, and he was looking at me like I was the one responsible, but I know I wasn't because I didn't eat anything on purpose knowing I was hella nervous and had a weak stomach and was stressed already. When his mom dropped me off, he gave me a peck and a hug good night. I remember skipping upstairs while my mama watched. She was high, but she had a grin like she was so happy for me. I was so high off the little kiss he gave me that I wasn't even worried about my mom being high. I just went to my room and listened to some Mary J. Blige.

Chapter 11

A lot of things started changing for me as I got older. I was still working with Bill off and on, but I knew he was about to let me go because once kids got to a certain age, he didn't want them to work for him anymore. At that point, they're not charming and cute; they're just challenging teenagers who only want to smoke weed—that's what he thought anyway—so I started looking for different jobs while still continuing to work for him. I was already two steps ahead of him on finding another job because I knew he wanted newer, cuter kids who were about to kill the Teen Leaders of California Club. I made Bill kind of mad at me because sometimes I told him I had to do other things when he came to pick me up, but he still made his money. He was a hustler and definitely was a great male role model, whether he was profiting or not. I still didn't mind giving him the money at the end of the day because he was helping me help myself by teaching me to have the guts to ask for a contribution. I worked with him from about eleven to thirteen or fourteen when I started my first internship at Highland Hospital after moving to West Oakland. So much was happening in so little time.

One day after I came home from working for Bill, I went upstairs on 61st and opened the door to see my cousin, Johnisha, and my nieces. She needed to live with her sister at that time down the street on Bromley in seminary, so I knew she was going through a lot. I loved my cousin so much, and she was really trying to find her way. I was a first-hand witness to a lot of the things that she went through. Johnisha was the daughter of my Auntie Stephanie, and when my auntie was killed, Johnisha was only nine months old and her big sister only eight. They moved to New Mexico with her dad, and she grew up with him and her stepmother, Denise. I loved Miss Denise. She had a beautiful soul, but that didn't save Johnisha from looking for love in all the wrong places. However, at the same time, she had my auntie's spirit, so she did not take any shit. She definitely was a tomboy, and she was attending Kids Mac, a junior high school in West Oakland, so Nisha was looking for God, and she'd asked me to go to church with her.

One day we walked to ShopRite, where my dad used to do his recycling with my Uncle Don selling little merchandise and having yard sales. As we got close, she noticed there was a church across the way. I was eating some hog head cheese, and my cousin just walked across the street without me. I didn't know what she was doing, so I followed her into the church. I remember walking in and seeing "CCC Cannon Christian Covenant Baptist Church" on the sign. It was right across the street from another church that used to have some good choir music. We could've gone to any church she wanted to go to, and the church with the choir was bumping, but something told her she needed to go to this one. Perhaps it was God.

As soon as we walked in, everybody stared at us. When we sat down, the preacher started speaking, and I could tell Johnisha was trying to translate his message to everything she was going through. I really wanted to support her, but I didn't know that I was supporting both of us at the time. Well, God was supporting both of us at the time. After the preacher finished, we were about to leave when a lady stopped us and asked us what our names were and why we came to the church. My cousin said she really didn't know, but something told her to come in because she was having a hard time. The lady hugged her and told her that it was going to be all right. She was at the right place at the right time, and everything happens for a reason.

The woman's name was Simone Parker, and I mean this lady was godsent. She'd been through so much. She immediately started telling us her life story and how she'd struggled in everything she's been through and how that made her overcome all the obstacles she'd encountered. She asked us if we wanted to be a part of the church and said she'd do her best to help with Bible study and regular church sessions. From that day on, she started picking us up and taking us to church and getting us more involved with the word of the Lord. One day, she dropped us off at my house on 61st, and I came to find out Simone and my mom were in the same program when my mom was trying to get clean. That made Simone want to help our family even more because she knew what my mom was going through, and she knew my mom wasn't clean yet, too. Plus, she really loved my brothers, Ray Ray and Keshad.

We started getting more involved with the church, and we became saved, so we had to get baptized. I remember my cousin going through the experience. It was kind of scary because she caught the Holy Ghost, and that was the first time I'd ever seen somebody behave like that. Even though I felt the Holy Spirit whenever I listened to gospel music, I'd never seen somebody be taken by the

Spirit in that way, but I loved that for Johnisha because I knew she was going through a lot and she needed to heal. She knew God was the only one who could do that for her.

Mama Simone had a lot kids. She had mostly girls and one boy. I remember going over to her house and spending the night often. I used to be kind of ashamed because I knew she was taking care of us and having to feed us as well as her other kids, but Mama Simone made me so happy. She also raised her kids to be independent. My hair was super damaged, so she had a few of her daughters care for it. I even used to wear some of their clothes. One daughter was close to my age. Her name was Aaliyah, and she was cool. We sang songs together and met with boys at the park together. I remember texting this boy who was seventeen, even though I was really young, and one of her sisters asked to use my phone. She wound up looking through my messages because I thought she needed to use my phone, but she was just trying to see who I was messaging. I really appreciated it later on because that meant she was looking out for me as a good sister, even though there were many times I felt out of place with them, but Mama Simone would always reassure me that we are all God's children, and nobody is better than anybody else. However, I still felt lower than them because my mom and dad were on drugs and Simone was fully in recovery and into the mission God set out for her, so I never got that close to Simone's kids. I remember really getting into it with one of the younger cousins because she was making me feel less than, and I got tired of it, so I got up in her face and was yelling and screaming at her. I remember Aaliyah intervened and stood up for her. I felt like they were about to jump me because I was standing up for myself. I understood why Aaliyah did it. I mean, I wasn't her real family, but I felt very hurt because the cousin kept on antagonizing me and teasing me about my mom being on crack, and I couldn't take it anymore, so I was willing to fight. At that point, I had already told one of Simone's oldest daughters what was going on because I felt like I could talk to her about a lot of things without being judged, and I think she told her mom about my being teased. Simone called both Aaliyah's cousin and me into the room and sat us down and told us that just because my mom was on drugs and her mom wasn't didn't make her any better than anybody else because you never know what happens in life.

My siblings and I used to have such a good time over at Mama Simone's house because she had so many kids, and everybody had their own things going on, so it was really easy for us to have fun and not need to be checked on so often. Plus Mama Simone had a lot of trust in her kids. I believe a lot of her kids could sing really well, and she made us go to choir rehearsal every week she was not playing. Ray Ray knew how to sing really well, so he had his own solo song, "Ain't No Rock." He sang the song so perfectly, and he was so cute when he thanked everyone. Everybody at church loved him, and the older folks couldn't get enough of him.

I love when they'd sing solos. Brianna she had one of the most beautiful voices to me, and Mama Simone's oldest daughter Simone was also in the choir. She had her mom's namesake, so people called her Duke. She was going through a lot in her life at this time as well, but she always stayed positive no matter how crazy things got for her. She knew God had her back. That's how much Mama Simone instilled God in all her kids.

At this time, Mama Simone was right by Arroyo, so everybody who went to elementary and middle school with me used to be up there by her house. I remember always seeing Christian and Sandy. They also used to go to church with us, but at that time I stopped liking Christian. It was just puppy love. As a matter of fact, most of the lovers I had in my younger days were just the result of puppy love, but I know I made all of these boys I loved feel so special because I loved so hard. Even if I really didn't know what love was at the time, I knew what I wanted to feel. Christian was also Briana's cousin, so I really couldn't like him like that because it felt like he was my sister's cousin, and that was too weird. And when I say Briana, I mean my first best friend from Elmhurst, Shon's daughter, or now you guys know her rather as big booty Bri.

Mama Simone treated us like her own kids. I really think she saw something in us that nobody else saw. She knew we were so special. I remember going on all the same trips she took her kids—vacations, birthday parties, hotels. She always made sure Sunday dinner was on before she went to church, so everybody could eat, and she could cook so well. I loved Mama Simone's food. When we moved to West Oakland, we started seeing each other less and less because Simone was sick, and I didn't even know it. It was like she just stopped seeing us, and I was going through so much shit in my life at the time that I couldn't always make it to East Oakland because I was too far away. We used to have to catch the bus all the way from West Oakland to downtown from downtown to East Oakland on the 82L.

KASANDRA JOHNSON

We used to go to parties, and they used to be lit as fuck. At this one party, I'd even broken the door because I was working somebody so hard. The lady the house was so mad, but nobody told on me because they wanted me to dance with them. Mama Simone let us have our freedom, but at the same time she didn't play, and I was always honest with her. I had special talks with her about my life and what I wanted to be and what I wanted to do, and she encouraged me by saying I could do whatever I wanted to do and I could be whoever I want to be. She said it was all up to me and how I chose my path. My cousin Nisha on the other hand was a little older, and she was already doing what she wanted. She had issues with authority, and she wanted to do only what she wanted to do at the time. I remember one time my godmother asked Johnisha if she wanted to stay with her. Johnisha said no because she wanted to come into the house whenever she wanted. Basically she didn't want to have a curfew, and Mama Simone didn't say anything about it. We studied all types of things in Bible study. From the New Testament to the Old Testament, Simone really broke the Bible down for us and taught us about all of the different stories. She showed us what happens from the beginning to the end when Jesus comes back and we need to be safe and free of sin. Even though Mama Simone was very religious and into her Bible, she also allowed her kids to do regular kid stuff, and that's what I really loved about her. We celebrated every holiday including Halloween, and she let her daughters have little boyfriends and enjoy their lives. I really admired that. One of her daughters had started making some money braiding hair, but she was braiding so much she hurt her fingers. One day, Simone told her she needed to take a break, that it didn't matter if she needed money or not, her health and her fingers were more important than whatever she was trying to purchase.

Mama Simone made sure all of the kids were taken care of, so there weren't any problems. Ray Ray was really close with Brandon, the son of my godmom. They used to be hella bad together. They rode their bikes everywhere and got into it with everybody. They were the typical little rascals of East Oakland and would also hang out with Christian and Sandy sometimes. I remember Brandon having dogs and always playing with them. I think one of the dogs bit him just because he would play too much with them. Brandon was the fool and he always had everybody cracking up. I think I might've been the closest to Brandon just because he was the only boy in his family and I was the only girl in mine. He was also down to earth, almost acting like an old man at times. I love my Mama Simone so much. She really gave me a lot of strength to keep pushing.

I was very hurt when I found out she passed away from cancer. God put that lady in my life for a reason, even though at the time, I didn't understand it, but she did, and I'm really thankful for that. I'm not that close to her kids, but I still want them to know how grateful I am. I know they're aware their mama was so amazing. I'm sure they have a bond that could never be broken because of Simone Parker.

Simone also had a husband named Melvin who was a mailman. My mom told me he was the mailman for her grandmother, so he'd been working with the post office for a long time. From what I understood, Melvin was a deacon at the church. I wasn't allowed to speak with him, but I didn't care because I was a child and I'd seen him at church with Simone often. I didn't see a lot of men in church with their wives, so that meant a lot to me despite whatever they went through that made him a God-fearing man because he was willing to give his life to the Lord. That's how I knew I wanted a man that was close to Christ.

Chapter 12

I didn't have a lot of friends on 61st, so my mom sometimes made me go down the street to play with this girl, but I hated to play with her because she was stingy all the time. Her daddy had a hell of a lot of money and she was the only child, so she really didn't understand what it was like to have to share. I stopped playing with her, and she was mad when that happened, but she quickly became sad because she realized I was a good friend. I didn't even want to go over to her house when she had a big event. She later apologized, but our friendship was never the same because she knew my mom smoked crack, and she said something to me that was very hurtful. I don't think she meant to say it, but it affected me, and that was the beginning of my saving my energy by not talking to her ever again. It got to the point that if somebody made me really mad, I realized I had the power to either entertain the bullshit or just simply walk off and not say anything. I learned that's what hurt people the most: when I'd boss up and prove them wrong, especially when I've been nothing but good to a person. That happened to me with a lot of people, and that's why I put up my guard each time. I didn't like to be mean, and I never wanted to make people feel bad. I was just protecting my energy because I didn't want to get hurt. My patience for people wasn't the same patience people had for themselves, and it took me a long time to understand it because I was so passionate about the people I loved. Later on I realized I have to love myself; I have to put all of my energy into myself because sometimes people don't appreciate it. They may appreciate me later, but in those moments they didn't. I'm also a strong believer that everything happens for a reason, so maybe in the end I helped them, but all in all, I'm pretty sure the people who wronged me regret every second they wronged me. It takes a lot for me to just stop talking to people because I'm an empathetic person, but if it gets to a point where that happens, it means I don't want to beat their ass. I won't want to kill them as long as they don't put their hands on me. I show people respectfully how a boss moves.

While catching the bus to school from 61st, I was always three minutes late because it often came a little later, so either I was going to be early or I was going to be a little late. However, I always turned in all of my work, and I always scored high on my tests.

THE STRUGGLE THAT MADE ME

There were two principals, who were the same ones who ran the school when my brother went to Elmhurst, so they thought I was going to be troublesome, but they knew Major was smart, so they knew all my mom's kids were going to be as well, but Major left a bad taste in their mouths, so I had to really prove myself. I had to show them that I was capable even though I wasn't as bad a Major, but at least they knew I was smart as hell.

I remember Major telling me that when he went to Elmhurst, they had a big talent show. That's when we had a ball and were in bangles. We wore singles, and I had the ponytail that went down my back like a sack of potatoes. We went through a lot of fashion trends through the late '90s and early 2000s. It was so cool because Elmhurst had a culture where we as students could actually dance and be ourselves. There were the two different schools, but I liked the fact that they allowed students to live in a culture of hip-hop dancing together. That was very important to young Black people back then. People used the turf and would win tofu Friday, so I started to think it was kind of like a clown dancing. They used to go crazy like it was a type of art where dancing looked like they were painting a picture, and I loved that. I loved to see the animation of Black people and how they naturally move to the rhythm.

I remember my Uncle John staying with us on 61st. I loved my Uncle John despite some of the things he did. I was always his Kiki Bug, and he always embraced me so dramatically. He made me feel like a little princess. Uncle John was my cousin Johnisha's father, but she stayed with her big sister Delana before coming to live with us. Delana already had a lot of things going, plus Johnisha wasn't trying stay with my granny Sandra in the West Oakland Acorn High Rises. Johnisha's dad came to visit her over at my house every now and then because Uncle John went back-and-forth between Oakland and New Mexico. I could tell Johnisha was trying to rebuild a relationship with her dad regardless of what people said about him or how anybody felt about him. My cousin Nisha loved her dad, especially considering she didn't have her mom, but my uncle was a challenging character. Every chance he got, he stole for his people to eat. He did some fucked up shit, but through his addiction, he never left his daughter. But sometimes she didn't want to call because my uncle could be a bit violent. One time, someone called him a name, so he punched the man so hard in the face, the guy though he'd lost his eye. He was looking on the ground asking, "Where my eye at?"

KASANDRA JOHNSON

My Uncle John was a thief. He was sick, but I don't really hold anything against him. When somebody's sick, you can't really be mad at them. My mama knew my uncle stole any time he came around, so it was funny how she prepared. It really reminded me someone of Friday. Anytime we'd see him coming, we'd have to hide our shit because he was definitely going to take something. Most of the time, we didn't give a fuck because it was just spare change. My Uncle John loved some change.

My Uncle John made the best omelets because he used to go to ShopRite and bring back cookies and eggs and cheese. He used to make us omelets and bake amazing cookies. Everybody called him shystie, but if someone fucked with us, he definitely made sure we were good. I could only imagine the love he had for my Auntie Stephanie Zeno, and I'm sure it took a lot to open up a strong hearted woman like that. My Uncle John had to be special to my auntie. I know the pain my uncle felt when she passed was hard to handle, especially having to raise a nine-month-old, but Johnisha had a lot of mother figures who guided her and Mama Simone was certainly one of them.

I remember my godmother Shon coming to pick me up around the time I lived on 61st. I would have my stuff packed and ready. I had to have a lot of panties and bras because every time I knew I'd be staying there for more than a week. I loved going over to Briana's house even though she moved like ten times in two years, so it was really hard for me to keep up with her. On top of that it seemed like she was moving further and further away each time. At one point, she moved all the way to Stockton, and I wasn't able to visit her as often, but we still talked on the phone and kept in touch in the evening. We still went to the same school; I just couldn't spend the night over at her house.

At this point, my dad was whipping us less because we were getting older, but he'd just beat us harder because he really wanted to make a statement and he wanted to have that power. I'd try my best not to get in trouble, and it helped that I was moving around a lot in my life. It was kind of hard for my dad to beat my ass because I was always at a friend's house.

We had all types of people stay with us on 61st including my Uncle Ernie. One time, Major came home to visit with a bankroll of twenties, and he was flashing it down the street, just tapping and talking shit. We walked by some seminary guys in an old school weed van, and two of them bounced out. My heart started beating really fast. One instantly gave me a look to run as if they

THE STRUGGLE THAT MADE ME

were going to try to rob Major, but in my heart I didn't care what he told me to do. I would have gotten my ass beaten, too, but they wound up just telling Major to be careful flashing his money like that because it could get stolen. Another time Major got hella drunk and passed out, so my Uncle John painted his fingernails pink. It was really funny because Major woke up super mad, but he should've understood he shouldn't get caught sleeping because it could've been worse. I loved when my brother came home. I felt so protected. At this point, we were fighting and still arguing as Virgos. We used to clash on just about everything, but I started doing my own thing and found my own way, and he kind of admired that and left me alone. When he left to go to my uncle's brewhouse, I was so mad he had to go because we were just getting to a good place in our lives and our relationship.

As soon as he moved, I felt like somebody was watching me walk around in the house. I didn't pay much mind to that, though. One day, I joined Ray Ray in the TV room. At the time, we only had one TV with cable to watch the Disney Channel. I was watching this movie called *Jump In!* with Corbin Bleu, who had curly hair and looked like he was biracial. We didn't have roaches on 61st, but we did have an ant problem. Anytime we left something sweet out, the ants would fuck that shit up. At some point, my mom had a lady come in to clean our every week. After the movie, I went in my room to write some poetry about how I was feeling and what I was going to do. I had a diary that I kept at the end of my bed, and nobody knew about it. Auntie Erica gave it to me and told me to write my feelings down whenever I was feeling like I needed to talk or get something out. I heard a knock at the door, so I hid my diary under my bed as my dad came in. He asked what I was doing, so I told him I was getting ready to sleep, but I could tell something was wrong because he never came in like that. I thought I was going to get a whooping for something I did at school or to somebody around the neighborhood, but that wasn't the issue. He had a whole different look on his face that I'd never seen before. He told me he loved me so much and no matter what happened he wanted me to take care of my mom and my brothers. He started crying uncontrollably, and that was the first time I'd ever seen my daddy cry. He'd always been strong; he always knew how to fight. I didn't understand why he was crying. He tried to explain that everything was going to be okay but that he was about to leave. He said that if he didn't come back, he loved me so much and he never wanted me to forget what he taught me. He said he was fighting to protect his family by making money. I remember the whole conversation, and I knew something was wrong. I felt like something bad was about to happen to my dad. He was talking tags, but I knew in my heart something was about to happen. After he talked to me, he wiped his face and mine and told me to get some rest. When he opened the door, I saw two men in suits who reminded me of *Men in Black*. They looked like agents, and I couldn't help but get up, but my dad told me to go back in the room and that everything would be alright. I didn't have any understanding of what was going on; I didn't know who these people were; I didn't know what they wanted; all I knew was I was ready to fight for my dad. As much as he beat my ass and put me in a corner and gave me lecture after lecture because he was drunk, I still didn't give a fuck. I didn't want my daddy to get hurt no matter what he'd done. There were so many thoughts racing through my head. I thought maybe he owed the dope dealers some money because my parents would always have to rob Peter to pay Paul, and if my dad made less than he spent, how was he ever going win.

As the men walked my dad out, I saw my mom coming from the back of their bedroom. My mom and my dad had the last room down the hall, and it was hella big, too. I also saw my mom behind her with her phone to her ear. My mom was hella mad that these men fucked up her high, and she was talking a lot of shit to them trying to explain that this was her house and she didn't know why they were in it. I could tell she had been drinking and smoking, but she cranked her game all the way up. I was so terrified every minute of every second I thought about my dad. I wondered if he was going to make it back home. Muslims were standing by the door, so we couldn't get out at this point, and my brothers knew something was going on, too. I couldn't hide my fear anymore.

When my dad came back I remember the police showing up about five minutes after. They bounced out the car and yelled if anybody named Rochelle was there. My mama instantly looked around and said, "Hell no, that ain't me." The police officer asked if everything was okay, and the leader of the Muslims stated that this was his house and that we were falsely renting it out. All of the sudden, about fifteen Muslims came out of nowhere in suits. They had been surrounding the whole house. We walked downstairs outside in a line—my little brother, my baby brother, and me. I was so terrified because all of the Muslims had guns and they moved so militantly. I was so mad Major wasn't there and had only just left, but at the same time, I was happy because I knew he wouldn't have taken any of this well. The police calmed everyone down, and I was so happy when all of those Muslims left. My mom got everything out of the house that same night, and we left and never came back. We were forced to live with my granny at the Acorn High Rises.

A lot of my family stayed with us on 61st as well. My Uncle John, Auntie Stephanie's boyfriend before she passed away, and my Uncle Ernie stayed with this us often no matter the house we lived in. Major would still come home every now and then to check on us, but he was slowly fading because he was fully living with my Uncle Donald at this point. My older brother Greg was in and out of programs and was down the street trying to get his life together, but he would always come visit us, too. My mom actually started renting the house out from someone who ran one of his programs, but he wound up being a fraud. We learned that the house we lived in actually belonged to a Muslim family, and one leader's name was Yusuf Beh. A lot of people know them from the bakery they owned along with a lot of other businesses. There were some good Muslims and some bad Muslims. They had a lot of brothers, and it was only by the grace of God that we made it out of that predicament without anybody getting hurt. That was the last day we stayed on 61st before moving to West Oakland.

Our Mexican neighbors next door on 61st lived in a Victorian house, and I felt weird about that because it seemed too good to be true. It was a four-bedroom, three-bathroom house, and it had a huge basement. I remember us kids going downstairs to see what was there, and it was full of a bunch of antique Muslim things. There were also clothes that looked like they came from Africa, but I never thought they were from the black Muslim bakery.

Part II
Welcome to West Oakland

Chapter 1

Moving to West Oakland changed my life. To make it out of West Oakland without being a snitch, a sucker, or a bum, you have to be a bad person. West Oakland opened my eyes to how to play the game. I learned about a lot of politics in West Oakland, and I started understanding the dynamics of the institutional oppression set up in the area. We all were crammed in at my granny's two-bedroom apartment at the high rise. It was bad enough she loved to keep antiques and collectibles, and our Section 8 voucher was running out, so we didn't have a lot of time to find a place, which is how we wound up living on Chase Street. I'll talk to you more about that later on in the book.

I was still going to Elmhurst, but I was about to transition to Cole Middle School because my mom was tired of giving all of us bus and lunch money. Even though I still was working for Bill at this time, I was going through a lot after being traumatized by the Muslims, and I kind of stopped working slowly. I remember everybody was so sad that I was about to leave, but at the same time, a lot of people were happy because I fucked with a lot of kids. We never really went outside at first because we didn't know anyone, and honestly, we were going through a lot collectively. My granny was never home because she was dating this man named Danny in Modesto at the time, but even though she was gone, we still had to make sure the house was clean because my granny loved to fuss. My granny was good, but when she wanted to fuck with someone, she would fuck with him to the max, and that's why my mom tried her hardest to hurry up and find a place to move to. She hated being without a home. She wanted to be comfortable on her couch in peace.

Sometimes we went outside to play on the playground downstairs. I remember staying out often, and that's when Johnisha used to stay with my granny all the time while going back and forth from New Mexico. We'd sit down on the playground, go in the laundry room, or just lounge around with my cousin. She was dating a couple of boys at the time, and I remember we used to sing and make dances together. I used to love the song "Be My Ride or Die Chick" by Go Dav that went like this:

"Why do you do the things you do just for me? While niggas hated, by my side you stayed. And you did that for me when you didn't have to. For that I love you. You trusted me. I trusted you. You confide in me. I confide in you... For me you'll ride or die. I look in your eyes. I see the sunset tonight. Together forever, my baby..." (Go Dav, 2007).

My other cousin Delana also stayed with my granny, but at this time Delana had already gotten her housing and Section 8 voucher, and she was doing really well for herself. I remember Delana used to try to help me do my hair after teasing me about how torn up it was. I had a way of loving her family. She didn't mean any harm, but she was definitely brutally honest. She was another Virgo who didn't take any shit. Everybody thought she was a fighter, but she really was just a strong-minded person like me. Everybody thought I was a fighter, too, but I really was not. I just had to defend myself and didn't want anybody to keep fucking with me.

I remember when Ray Ray and I had one of our last fights. It was over at my granny's house after we'd moved in, and my granny was gone. My mom had left for the store, and my daddy was gone, too. Ray Ray and I were arguing over something, and we started fighting. I got the best of Ray Ray, and he got so mad that he went into the living room, grabbed the remote, and threw it in my face. My eyes started watering, and I couldn't even attack him anymore. He was so mad he called out my name in a rage. I couldn't even see, but I knew how mad he was and how much I'd triggered him. I didn't even want to fight him anymore or for him to call me a bitch and throw a remote at me as hard as he could. I knew I was doing way too much, so I got so quiet and so calm, but once he got to that point, it was over, so I tried to never get him that enraged again. We were getting older, and we were both young teens just trying to figure ourselves out. Our mama always taught us to stick together in a fight, however the advice was never for any of her kids not to fight one another. Later on, I saw why she said that because you can't let somebody hurt your family, and that was one thing I took seriously in Oakland. Anytime somebody fucked with my family, I really went off. Like I really didn't care that much if bitches lied about me. I gave them passes, but when it came down to my brothers, I didn't want them to feel like they didn't have anybody, even though I felt like I didn't have anybody a lot of time. I didn't care because I loved them more than I loved myself, and that's still true to this day.

One day, my mom asked Ray Ray to go to the store to get some milk and bread and a couple of other things. She really didn't like him going, but we caught the bus all the way from West Oakland to East Oakland often, so she trusted us enough to go to the store. She knew he wasn't going to bother anybody or get into it with anybody, or at least she knew that he wouldn't want to start shit. On my brother's way back from the store, however, neighbors from the high rise were watching him and wanted to steal whatever Ray Ray had purchased. I couldn't believe they took my little brother's stuff. I was so mad when Ray Ray came upstairs and told us what had happened to him, I went downstairs hella fast and stayed outside for about five minutes to see if they were going to come back, but they were gone. I was so upset my brother went through that, and he was hella mad, too. I could tell Ray Ray was traumatized, and I hated the sight of my brother so scared. I never wanted him to be scared of anything. I always felt like I needed to protect him by any means, and I didn't give a fuck how much he got on my nerves. Seeing him so distraught and scared like that made me really mad. I didn't even care about being in West Oakland. I knew I was going to catch whoever did this because West Oakland was small and at Acorn everybody knew everybody, so I knew the word was going to get around fast. I didn't know how fast, though.

One thing about West Oakland is there could be nobody outside, but if something started, about thirty seconds later everybody would come out of nowhere like roaches wanting to see Black people fight each other. But this didn't happen when Ray Ray was robbed. I really thought it could have been worse than it was, but by the grace of God, those kids didn't go any further than theft. But they didn't know who they were fucking with, and I told Ray Ray that the next time he saw them, he needed to not be scared. I told him to fight them. I didn't care if there were more of them even. Ray Ray was in shock when they'd jumped him, but he said he wasn't going to be scared anymore.

Every time I left the house, I was hoping I'd catch one of them. Ray Ray had already described to me what they looked like, and I'd seen them around before when I used to visit my granny's house from 61st. One day, Major came to visit us from Brentwood. He was about to move with my mom's younger sister to Berkeley. When my brother came back to visit us, it made me feel really safe and protected. He used to be so funny, and I used to love all his stories about all the places he went to with Uncle Boo and our other family members, even though sometimes I got jealous because he used to leave us and go to places the rest of us had never gone to. The only time I wasn't happy for him, though, was when he went to Usher's concert on my birthday. I was so mad because I loved Usher, but I could tell he felt bad for leaving us home. He wanted us to understand traveling and experiencing life on another level, so when we could take his place, he let us, but for the most part he was experiencing these trips for himself, and my mom didn't have a lot of money for us to go all at the same time. I was really happy for my brother because I felt like he deserved to go places and do things. I feel like everybody deserves to travel and see the world.

When Major came to visit, we told him how Ray Ray got jumped walking to the store for my mama and how he was so anxious to go outside and back to the store now. Major happened to bump into the little boy who was with the crew who stole from Ray Ray, so Major asked the kid if he could go get whoever had jumped his brother. Major came back upstairs and told me that the boys who jumped Ray Ray were about to come and we had to fight. I was so ready and so anxious to see who'd touched my brother, who'd put fear in his heart. I want to fuck them up one by one. I didn't give a shit if they were girls or not. I was going to protect my brother because I'd never seen him like that, and I wanted to show him that he didn't have to be scared of anybody. I was his big sister.

Major mentioned a little girl was also around and she said she didn't care if Major went to go get his sister, so that's exactly what he did. I was so ready to beat this girl up. I was planning out everything wanting to use all of the homemade boxing lessons my daddy gave me. I was angry, and I wanted to whoop somebody's ass. I already was fighting, but nobody in West Oakland knew me. They didn't know me from a can of paint. All they saw me do was help my granny get in and out of the apartment with groceries. I was quiet until someone fucked with my family. My mama put Vaseline on my face and tied up my one month-old hairdo. I had on a Dallas jersey that my granny had given my dad and some leggings. I don't even remember what type of shoes I had on; I probably was barefoot. We were in a rage before we went downstairs. My dad told Ray Ray he better fight them and he better not be scared. He didn't have to be scared because his family was there, and we weren't going to let anything happen to him. I could tell Ray Ray was scared, but at the same time he had to do what he had to do. He was mad, but he really didn't want to fight. It really didn't affect him until he actually started fighting the little boy when we went downstairs. Initially, we didn't see anybody, but we were ready. Major, Keshad, my mama, my daddy, and I were prepared.

Finally, somebody came from the other side of the fence and asked who we were looking for. It was the same girl who was talking shit to Major, telling him to go get his sister. Major said, "We're looking for you. You wanna say 'go get yo sister?' Well, she's right here."

I started pacing back-and-forth with the fence against my head. I told her to come around or I was ready to jump over. The girl said, "Oh no, I didn't say that. My cousins jumped y'all. That wasn't my brother, so they don't have nothing to do with me, but I'm a go get them for you."

I didn't give a fuck who it was at this point. I just wanted to fight, and that girl damn near ran back inside her house and told the little boy to come outside. Ten minutes passed, but we waited patiently. When the boys finally came outside, they were acting like we were the ones who jumped them. There were three little boys, and I wanted to go at them, but my daddy said no. Ray Ray was going to fight them one on one. I was so mad because I'd never even experienced getting jumped in East Oakland. We'd only ever fight one on one, so I really didn't understand why they wanted to jump my little brother. I wanted them to feel his pain so badly.

They started fighting, and at first, it didn't look like they were even fighting. They were just leaning toward each other like in the NFL. I was getting hella mad, telling Ray Ray to takeoff on him. The other little boys were egging on the other boy, Owen, to beat my brother up like he had before. That made me hella mad, so I quietly told Major I couldn't take it and I was going to have to get on one of the boys. Major said to do what I gotta do. I knew Major really didn't want me to takeoff on those boys because we were in their domain, but my brother knew that if I didn't do it then, some shit would go down while he wasn't there. So, he quietly nodded and gave me the okay.

One of the little boys knew I was coming, but he didn't know how hard I was coming. I fucked that little boy up, and the first couple hits he felt for sure. Then I slapped him and started trying to stomp his ass. After I start slapping him, Major tried to break it up while my daddy was still watching Ray Ray fight the other boy. My mama was on the side smoking a cigarette, calmly stating those boys had fucked with the wrong family.

My mom had a past in West Oakland, and she made it out by the grace of God, but it felt like a reincarnation to wind up there all of a sudden. After all she did to get herself out, I know she felt really bad for moving back, but at the same time, I knew she was prepared for whatever West Oakland threw at us. My mom told us there was always going to be somebody bigger and better than us, but as long as we held our own, nobody was going to fuck with us, and that's what I had in my blood. I couldn't help it. It wasn't like I was a bully at this time because I definitely understood what pain was, and I didn't want to keep putting people through that. So, I started trying to be positive, but it seemed like every time I would try to be good, something or somebody would try to throw me off, and I would really go off. Later on, I learned how to turn off my energy and not let people take so much of my power.

After I beat the fuck out of the little boy, the other little boy wanted to jump in, but he was so in shock that I was beating his friend up that he was just talking hella shit, trying to still be hard, and that shit made me mad, too, so I socked him in the mouth. He started crying instantly, and my family all laughed. At that point, they started saying they were going to come back with a big cousin to kill us. Major started laughing even more and told them we lived in apartment 205. I don't know why he told them that. Like why would you tell them the exact apartment we lived in? I was so mad, but at the same time, I really didn't give a fuck because whatever was going to happen was going to happen to us as a family, and we definitely stood strong and tall no matter what. We were ready for whatever.

My brother didn't even leave that time because he knew somebody or something was going to happen. At that time, he was about to try to graduate high school, but there were so many things holding him back from graduating. I remember he told me he wanted to be a radiologist and was in a program at Highland Hospital. I later joined that program after I worked for Bill because I had an interest in taking care of people, but I later on found out that I had a weak stomach and didn't like blood, so I couldn't get that little stipend money even if I wanted to. All of this was okay because God has something way better planned for me, and I couldn't even imagine all of these things that were going to happen to me. I didn't understand why I was going through so much, but at the end of the day, I have so much faith in myself.

We went back upstairs to reevaluate what had happened, and my mom wanted to call my granny to tell her everything because we were living in her house. There were five of us, not including my grandma, living in a two-bedroom apartment, so my mom didn't want to call her and report any problems or incidents, but my mom knew something was about to happen. She was scared, but she didn't show it. About thirty minutes later, we got a knock on the door, and it was the same little boy who told us he was going to get his cousins to come kill us. Major already had his shoes on, and I think he even had a gun, but my mom wouldn't let him bring it. I was really mad because I thought something bad was going happen to my brother, so I wanted to go downstairs to win. I didn't give a fuck what was going happen, but as soon as the little boy said his cousins were coming, Major flew downstairs like a bird. From what I understood, the two boys were in the laundromat, and they did have a gun. Major had out his own. I remember his coming upstairs like two minutes later saying he beat the fuck out of them.

Some time passed and we heard another knock. My brother was about to answer the door again, but my mama got in front of him and begged him not to. As soon as she said that, a gun went off. It was only one good shot. I wasn't even scared; I still was just hella mad, but I was happy my brother had come back upstairs so the fear of his getting shot was over. My granny' door was shot by a little paper.

I know a lot about guns, and even though it was just a little pepper, those shots can bounce around in your body and will fuck your insides up. If Major had been hit with that, I'm sure it wouldn't have been pretty.

Chapter 2

I knew a lot about the streets and politics and how everything moved, but I wasn't involved, and this book is not to talk about specific gangs. [Dipset, Circle City, P-Team, Dog Town, Delete Team, Lady Gas, Lady Team, Bolly Girls, D.N.I, STI, Milliton Girls]—yeah, I know all of the gangs. This isn't about anybody or games. This book is to bring awareness that this shit has to stop.

I just want to give you guys a little insight on how much I really knew about gangs. I was in a couple, but I only was in a gang to let bitches know I was a leader and not a follower. I didn't like head games and how girls had leaders. I was a leader in my eyes regardless, so joining a gang was never about trying to suck up to my friends because I really couldn't care less. I was the only girl, so I was used to being alone. Bitches were later intimidated by me because they didn't understand why I loved to be around all of the boys and play sports. They thought I was hella fast, but I really didn't lose my virginity until late. Even at the schools I went to, people thought I was fucking all the little boys I talked to, but I really wasn't at the time. I just was very affectionate because I've always been around that with my mom and dad. They've been together for about thirty years and married around that same age, so I've always seen them together and I've always wanted what they have, even though they had their ups and downs. I always knew I wanted to be married but with the right person.

Major stayed with us for a more couple days before going back with my Auntie Teisha in Berkeley. He was still working on some personal shit, but at the same time, he tried to make sure we were good no matter where he was. My mama was really trying to find a place for us to live at this point because there was too much going on and everybody knew where we were staying. People knew my granny would never be in town, and they knew we were new. When it was summertime, it was so hot that we were forced to go to Acorn's pool. I knew some of the other kids, but they didn't really know me because I was the new face.

I was a little girl, so I wasn't intimidating at all, but I was hella bad trying to get high with little boys and rap because that was my passion. I always looked up to girl rappers like Trina and Remy Ma and later Nicki Minaj and Cardi B. I also loved listening to R&B female artists like Keyshia Cole, Beyoncé, and Keri Hilson, as well as older pop and blues singers like Whitney Houston, Mariah Carey, Diana Ross, and Patti LaBelle. My granny used to always play music oldies and goodies. One of her favorite songs was Mind Playing Tricks on Me by Ghetto Boys.

My granny was the matriarch of our family on my dad's side. Sandra K. Toliver had been through so much and overcame so much hardship. She struggled from losing my auntie when she was knocked out of a tree or a three-story glass window. My daddy was two years old, and she was still selling drugs and dating the big dope man. I loved when my granny used to get drunk because she would literally rip her twenties, fifties, and hundred-dollar bills and make us put them together to take them to the bank. My granny had all different types of jewelry and cars. She sold a gang dope, and all her boyfriends were real dope men. One of my granny's best friends was actually my great auntie, Eloise, who was my mother's auntie.

My Auntie Eloise was cold. She had a house in North Oakland right by a bar, and she threw parties every weekend. She worked for Lillian's, and she had money. She owned her own business and house, in which my mom and dad got married in their ghetto fabulous wedding. I loved my Auntie Eloise's house because she had all different types of exotic things. I remember she had a stuffed panther, and I was scared of it, but Ray Ray was even more scared. I would laugh every time he got nervous. around it. My auntie also had a daughter named Vinetta P who changed her name to something from Africa. She'd seen a lot of bullshit, too, and people tried to bash her when she was just trying to figure herself out. People need to stop judging others just because they are trying to figure themselves out. There's no reason talk down on them. Everyone's human. Plus, I was very inspired by African culture. When she took me over her house I felt spiritually connected to my ancestors.

I went over to my Auntie Eloise's house once after I'd gotten my hair done across the street by some girl, who had a son who was a little person. That was the first time I'd ever seen a little person, and I was a little scared, but he was super nice. I'd never had a conversation with a little person before. I never thought of little people in that way. I never thought that they were actual people because I'd only seen them on TV. I thought they were actually Santa's helpers, but Sonoma's son made me realize there are little people who are older and more experienced than me. They are adults and you have to treat them with respect. I believe he was so nice because my granny told him he could watch me sing jazz, and he was ecstatic.

I would often write songs or poetry often in my diary. My Auntie Erica got me a diary to express myself because I would get my ass whooped every time I spoke the truth, so instead she recommended I write in the diary or on my old HP laptop. Once, Major looked through and told my momma. I would just write to write. Sometimes it didn't make sense, but as long as I got my thoughts out, it felt amazing to me in the moment. This is how I had to write this book. I literally just said everything over a long period of time. I lived in the moment and had so much anxiety. I had to look back at a lot of bad, traumatizing moments, but I also lived in great memories as well, and that is what this book is about. The good, the bad, and the ugly is really what I wanted to write. What I learned from the ugly is I have to read all of the signs God is giving me, but first, I have to understand that he's giving me the signs. I wasn't aware of any signs at this point in my life, however, God was always in my life, and he always was guiding me. I just didn't understand the path he was taking me on.

Chapter 3

I had to move schools from Elmhurst to Cole, and that was one of the hardest transitions of my life. I was alone. I didn't know anybody and nobody really knew me. All the credit I had built up in East Oakland didn't matter. It was a clean slate, and I had to reclaim my pride regardless of whoever saw me as weak or not. I always knew I had too much pride to let anybody fuck with me, even though I let a lot of people slide. Now I understand why God let me let them slide because I used to get so mad sometimes when motherfuckers would tease me or use subliminal messages. It really didn't matter, though. I just had to get to the point where I didn't give a fuck.

When I first walked into Cole Middle, I already felt like I didn't want to be there. It was a whole different atmosphere. It felt like nobody wanted to learn. Everybody was just trying to judge what other students had and roast each other. It was like a fashion show, and they all really didn't have any money, but they tried their hardest to make it seem like they were a celebrity or something. Middle school was the time I had to level up and really show people that I was ready for high school. Materialism was a dark thing. Students were always scamming. They had to look nice, but they didn't have a dollar in their pockets. It wasn't everyone, but some people took it seriously. It woke me up because in East Oakland I had a different style. West Oakland had a totally different style, so everybody knew that I was in from East Oakland. I even had bitches ask me what I had on because I was so East Oakland. I'd even use lingo from East Oakland, so as soon as I opened my mouth, other students knew I was from there. All it took was talking about banking bitches and throwing them bows.

I remember getting my schedule printed out and seeing who my teachers were. I had one teacher named Octotuba. She was a science teacher from Africa who always ate some nasty ass fish for lunch. She had her whole class gagging after lunch. I hated it because it affected her class, but I also loved to learn. It was kind of hard because she had an accent, but she was pretty good at teaching, even though students gave her a really hard time. Everybody gave the teachers a hard time.

I loved one of my math teachers named Mr. Brown. He was a tall African-American older man. Mr. Brown was very calm and firm when he spoke, and if you pissed him off, he would definitely read you your rights. Some students used to crack up in Mr. Brown's class, but he'd tell those ignorant little boys to leave unless they wanted to learn. Mr. Brown originally grew up in West Oakland and literally walked from his house to school. He was very inspiring. I always looked up to Mr. Brown, and he was very handsome for being older.

I also remember my English teacher, but I forgot her name. Nobody really liked her because she always gave people detention and called students' mothers, but she really cared for the kids. Whenever we did well, she would give us hot apple cider or cocoa. She was also disrespected often. I remember a kid even tried to put his hands on her, and that wasn't cool.

Teachers go through a lot, especially teachers in Oakland. They deal with so much. They have to be counselors, therapists, parents, and teachers on top of all of that. They should be paid one of the highest salaries in America, but they're paid less than 35,000 dollars annually. That's nothing. They need to be getting paid at least double that, especially considering they spent a lot of their salary on materials for their class. I can't understand the dynamics of that on top of all the stress that the kids used to put them under. Like come on, y'all. We definitely need to change our local laws, so we can invest more money into education. Teachers should be happy to come to school and not have to worry about bills. They should also be able to take vacations when they need to because they're dealing with so many students at one time. And a lot of these students come from trauma. They act out a lot, and I know this because I did the same.

As I got more comfortable at Cole, I started fucking with people, but it wasn't like at Elmhurst. I just used to be hella funny. A lot of the boys wound up liking me. I went out with a couple of them, and later on, one became my baby's father. I never thought he was going to be my baby's father at the time, but God works in mysterious ways, and out of all the boys at Cole, I wanted to experience a lot of my life with him.

I was very misunderstood in a lot of ways, but at the same time, the little puppy loves I had made a bunch of mistakes. I know for sure all of those puppies were looking so pitiful because they really fumbled in the relationship. I was trying to have something special with them, but I was looking for love in all the wrong places. However, God makes no mistakes, and even though I made a lot of mistakes myself, I learned from them pretty fast.

THE STRUGGLE THAT MADE ME

When you're young, all you know is the tingling you feel inside and out, and you just want to do something, but I'm telling you now that it's not worth it. Sex is not all that, and once I lost my virginity at fifteen, I found that out I should've waited. That is a little later on in the story, and I definitely want to tell you about that experience and how it affected me. I chose my baby's father initially because he was beautiful, but nobody really saw him the way I saw him. I loved the way he smelled because he didn't smell very often. He also had a sort of charming nose that nobody really noticed but me. He had messed up teeth, but there was something about his spirit I liked. I didn't fall in love with my baby's father until after Cole when I went to McClymonds High School. That is when I met him, and I really thank God for placing him in my life because he later gave me the most precious thing in the world, my son Ralph.

The first person I saw was this girl named Natara. She was in one of the teachers' classrooms, and we were talking. I sat by her instead of the popular girls who were very smart. I really loved the underdogs because I was an underdog, too. I definitely was a cool nerd and also a little gangster, so nobody really understood where I fit in, but I didn't care because I just did whatever I wanted to do, fitting in with whomever I fit in with.

At the time, I played basketball with the boys in the afterschool program with this director named Mr. M. He had an assistant named Kirby, and they did music together. I was so ecstatic when they did the afterschool program because it was a great outlet for me. but I read him from the moment I saw him. I loved his spirit. He was always fucking with me, and I think at first, he had a crush on me, but later on, we both decided we just wanted to become best friends. I also had another best friend named Nyla. We weren't cool at first, but we wound up getting very close because we both loved music. I remember we worked on this one song for hours, and it was a hit. That's one thing I liked about Oakland. People from Oakland know how to sing well, and they know good music. We are naturally artists from the time we're born and that's what people here need to understand: if you have a passion for something, keep going. The people at the afterschool program really made me feel like I was a part of a group and I belonged. We wrote a song for the whole school, but we performed it only when the principal wasn't around because there were curse words in it. I really loved that Mr. M would let me express myself.

One time, I wrote a rap for Mr. M, and he told me his honest opinion. He said I had so much potential; I could be greater than Remy, greater than Nikki, greater than all of them. He said I was unique but needed to stop cussing so much. I needed to add more action words to my vocabulary, so people could hear me because people are ignorant. He took time out to show me how to hold my breath before and after I spit my bars and how to intrigue audiences with my stage performance. Mr. M taught me a lot, and I really thank him for that. He saw I was a troubled, little girl and knew I had a passion for music, so he tried his best to always motivate me to do better. He said, "Whatever you do, just keep riding, and you're gonna get better and better."

Nobody really knew the potential I had but Mr. M at that point. I remember recording music at a studio with Semaj. Semaj became my best friend in a very unique was. We rested through music and he was one of the first people to introduce me in the Bottoms. I had so much music, I was going to put out a mixtape. Honestly, I had about fifty songs, but nobody knew about it. I just kept writing and rehearsing by myself. I was really about this shit and knew what I wanted in my life and what I wanted to become. We used to always write our raps down in class and do our work at the same time. I was so motivated. I was even more motivated knowing I had people who wrote music, too. My friends and I made this one song I particularly loved: "Lil' Kiki from the East. Yeah, you know that's me. I'll be walking around the street, make a bitch not speak. Yeah, she mugging, yeah, I could mug, too. Stomp yo head in the ground, and then I am through."

After I had read the first verse, it seemed like they were all trying to come out hella hard. Everybody killed that, even Semaj, and at the time, he was misunderstood by a lot of people. They really were confused, and when we performed, he gave people the opportunity to see him in another light. He really had gas despite his being different. He could really write. A lot of people are different and can really speak the truth when others are only saying shit.

We used to get so high. We were smoking ourselves through the roof when he had weed. I never could get high over my house or even go around my mama high because I didn't know if she was sober or not, so I stayed away because I wanted to enjoy myself. Even though Semaj was my best friend, he made me feel very insecure at times, and he belittled me even though he didn't mean to, but he really made me feel less than. One time, we went to the dinner dance together, but I didn't have any money, so his cousin who did hair gave me her address, and I felt so beautiful. We later got into it, and he said some hurtful things to me about my dress, and that made me not even want to wear it, but I wound up going to the dinner dance, and I liked it so much. The little boys wanted to take pictures with me all of a sudden. Even though I used to kick their asses in basketball, they were saying I went to hang out with this older boy after the dance. He was actually one of the older brothers of my classmate. He was in the tenth grade at the time, and I learned the only time an older boy liked me was when he saw me dressed up and pretty. We hung out after the dance and made out, but he didn't fuck me. I didn't lose my virginity to him, but just the thought of making out with somebody who thought I was cute for the day made me feel like Cinderella or something. I know he really didn't like me; he just wanted something out of me, but he didn't do anything.

He only went as far as touching my coochie, but that was it, and I'm so glad I didn't give him anything else because at the time, I was into this one boy named Brandon. I later regretted sharing anything with him after he turned to talk to one of my friends from East Oakland who I'd gone to school with. He really hurt my feelings, and when I found out, I was mad at my friend at the time. Later I realized she'd done me a favor and she was just being honest. I regret how I treated her over a silly boy. I called them both dirty and salty-necked, but I never really wanted to bash anybody. I never wanted to bash anybody for that because even if someone was dirty, I still liked them regardless. That's how solid I was.

I didn't care how people talked about others. If I liked someone, I liked someone, and that's some Virgo shit that's been instilled in me. Ultimately, that's how everybody should feel. No one should worry about what other people have or say because how they feel about can't change. I saw this boy's character and experienced how he didn't apologize or try to fight for me. As a matter of fact, he even told everybody I was a hoe and was dirty and all this other weird ass shit. It's crazy because I was so mad at the time I didn't even want to get even. I just didn't say anything else to him. I wound up later having a conversation with him about everything, and we even went up doing something lighter, but it was never the same. He really hurt me, and it was so crazy at the time because I could've talked to other boys at the dance instead, but one thing about me is if I'm talking to you, I'm only going to talk to you. You have my undivided attention.

We were all hella young back then, so everybody really liked everybody, but I knew in my heart I was already in love, and if people knew how genuine I was at the time, they'd know I would have already been married. But God does things for a reason, and I guess it wasn't the right time for me.

I also talked to another boy who was from out of town, and we kicked it off. Our little dirty asses were vibing, but I knew he wasn't the one for me. This is not to say he wasn't hella sweet because he definitely was, and he had a great heart and great personality, but at the same time, I knew he wasn't the one. There was another girl named Kia who was rapping with us at the time, and she came in with a whole other vibe. I loved her style. Everyone thought she was a cool kid, but she was a little nerdy, too. Still, she was with the shit, and she was hella friendly with this boy named Dante who lived across the street from me on Chase Street in the Lower Bottoms.

Chapter 4

I remember getting into it with a couple of people, but I don't really remember having any fights. There were definitely a couple of bitches that were nasty, dirty, and out of pocket. West Oakland is small, so there were a lot of bitches fucking with the same boys in competition with each other. I noticed the culture of West Oakland focused on status, so you had to look like someone worthy of respect to receive it, just like in any other city. There was a lot of good, bad, real and fake, and bitches were talking out of pocket, but there was some foul shit going on in the background, and I'm just so glad I wasn't sexually involved at the time.

One time, I got into it with this boy who was the type to watch everybody dress up every day and judge what they wore. If someone had awesome knockoffs or some dirty on his shoes, then this boy would call them out. At this point, I was still working for Bill, and he used to take us to a golf store where we bought a bunch of shoes for like a hundred dollars, like three pair of Nikes or fake Jordans. No one could really tell they were fake in my opinion, so I wore them to school, but the boy noticed they weren't genuine, and he started teasing me. At first, it didn't faze me, but the boy kept going on and on about it, so I start teasing his ass, and I could tell he was in shock because I was quiet and sneaky. I still was outgoing, but I wasn't as outgoing as other kids because I wasn't in my domain in West Oakland. I never stopped being myself, though, and that's what people didn't like and maybe were even intimidated. But at the same time, I am who I am. The boy who teased me about my shoes was someone I feel admired me, but at the same time, he wanted to text me to see exactly who I was. He was mad I started roasting him hella bad, and we were going back and forth for a while before he told me he was going to get his big sister on me. Little did he know, shit like that did not faze me. Somebody saying they'll get a sister on me is a welcome challenge. As long as nobody touched me, I was fine. Bitches could talk as much shit as they wanted, but I was so mad that boy was taking it so far. I told him I didn't give a fuck and to go get her. I was ready as much as I was scared. He was talking about how she was hella bigger than me, but went to McClymonds High School, so I let him know I wasn't going to back down. After that incident, we got into it a couple more times, but he never actually got his sister on me, and then eventually he stopped fucking with me.

I also got into it with this other boy who had thick ass glasses and said something to him, and he told me he was going to get his big cousin from Ghost Town to beat me up. I still didn't care, though. I wanted somebody to touch me so bad after all of the shit I was going through with people testing me. I did get into that fight at Acorn, but nobody knew that was me because a couple of years had passed, and even the people who knew about that fight didn't go to my school or they weren't in my age group. Those kids were my brother's age, so I don't know if they were going to West Oakland Middle School at the time or Martin Luther King, but at this point nobody knew me. Later on, I realized the bitches those boys were talking about didn't have any hands. The only exceptions were Mazionna, and a couple of other bitches, but I did not know of them at the time.

I initially met Tati and Mazionna shortly after moving from Acorn in the high rises to the lower bitter when my brother was playing with one of the neighborhood kids. I was coming in from outside, but I used to love fucking with my brothers and his friends. I didn't know who Ray Ray was hanging out with; I just remember playing with them with a belt acting like I was going to whoop them. It was all fun and games until Mazionna and Tati came to my door asking me if I was trying to beat their brother. I was thrown off, especially because I was in a happy mood. I wasn't bothered enough to fight either one of them, but after they shared their perspective, I realized I would have been mad if my little brother told me that, too, but at the same time, it's dangerous to go to random houses. You don't know what someone has. The encounter ended with Mazionna talking shit and walking off. I knew I wasn't trying to really hurt her little brother. If anything, I was treating her brother like I do mine. I was the type of person who liked to protect myself. I knew when I really needed to fight. I was definitely a little bitch, but people were still trying to figure me out, which is the reason we didn't fight.

I will be talking about all of the underdogs, all of the people who should've been respected even if people didn't respect them or feel any type of way about them, even if I got into it with them before or not. I'm going to share the solid times and the shit that really mattered to me because that's what this book is about. This book is about the people who helped me change my life and figure out my purpose even in this very moment while writing this book. It took me a long time to write this book because there was so much content, but the important parts are mentioned, both good and bad. I'm making a part two because there's so much other shit that happened. I want y'all to be able to go to seminars and hear me speak. I want to speak to the same haters that didn't want me to make it and thought I was going to become another statistic. They're going to read this book. They're going to watch my seminars. Would you listen to me speak? They'll see me give back to the community and watch me get famous. They're going to see me on Netflix sharing theories and in sitcoms and spinoffs. I'll show how amazing my family was. They're going to watch me get wealthy, and as long as this motivates them to do better and try to be better, then that's all that matters. I don't care who looks at me any type of way or how they feel about me because, at the end of the day, I'm special, and to write this book, I had to do a lot of healing, not just for me but for the people who didn't even know hurt me. I forgive all of y'all. It's so crazy because the people who shot my brother, or the alleged people, were gang affiliated. They shot my little brother Kenny Ray, and I will talk to you more about that in my second book. Some of the people who were charged with killing my brother or shooting my brother were the same people I remember going on a rail at Acorn and rapping to those same people. I shared my craft with them. It was not my head. My rhymes were a part of all the killing and my brother's shooting. They probably don't even know that I know it was them, but I'm sure they know now, and I really want to say this to them even though I'll express this again later in the book: I'm really not mad at you. I wanted to die when it happened, but if I knew the reason why it had to happen, I would not be telling this story, so I really thank you, and I hope you guys get closure because my family is healing, and I hope you can heal and still accomplish whatever you need to in the state that all of y'all are in. I can't get into a lot of details, but just know that I know exactly who shot my brother, and the people who were charged with it included you, but at the same time, I know the truth. They didn't take the deal already, and whether it was them or not, they chose to not say it wasn't them, and that is bittersweet because I understand that you're not supposed to snitch, but at the same time, I know the one who pulled the trigger. The man charged wasn't the one who pulled the trigger. It is what it is, though. My brother tried his best to identify exactly who did it, but it really didn't matter. It was done.

At Cole, I knew Nyla because she thought there was something going on between her boyfriend and me. She picked on me constantly, and eventually I snapped, I was so mad. The supervisor grabbed my hand as soon as we were about to fight and pulled me away from Nyla. As I was dragged away, she yelled "okay, Kasandra, you wanna fight? You wanna fight?"

I was so mad tears started coming down my face. I hated that I cried whenever I got angry, but after wiping my tears, I'd go crazy. When someone got me to the point of crying, there was no going back, but we had a low-conflict resolution and wound up not fighting. I realized we actually were similar in a lot of ways, and we became really close after we realized we both knew the whole Keyshia Cole album. I was so happy to come to school and finally make some friends who really understood me and my favorite music.

Nyla and I also hung out outside of school. We went to parties in East and West Oakland. She was my best friend. I can't say everything we did, but we definitely weren't taking shit from anyone. Nyla was in an out of living with her mom and this lady named Kat. I remember going over to her house a couple times. There was one night where her mama was yelling at us and her cousin. I loved Willy. Willy didn't play, and she also never took shit from anybody regardless of what she did or how she did it. It made sense to me later why Nyla acted the way she did and didn't take shit either.

A lot of the ladies in West Oakland were fighting and didn't know their worth, so I can imagine what young girls were going through at the time because I was going through a lot, too. Even though I was having sex, I still was going through a lot. I remember one time Nyla and I were...Nyla and I were in East Oakland May with these boys in the Alphabets. They were a little older, so we were excited and knew we had to dress up and act accordingly. That was one of the best nights of our lives because we were vibing with those boys. They were gentlemen even though they were gangsters in the streets, but at the same time, they didn't misuse us or take advantage of us. We might've had too much fun that night because we didn't notice our phones had died, and both of our parents were looking for us. We had to rush to West Oakland because it was getting hella dark. I remember walking up from the bus stop to Acorn with Nyla and seeing her mama and my mama. Both of them slapped the fuck out of us, and which we knew they were going to do, so we took the slaps.

THE STRUGGLE THAT MADE ME

We walked around the next day with our heads in the clouds thinking about these little boys. I don't think we even saw the boys again after that, but I remember I loved Willy and her daughter despite growing up in the Acorn projects. She wanted the best for her daughter, and if that meant leaving her with other people she knew could take care of her daughter better than she could at the time, she did it. I really admired that about her, not to mention she was not to be fucked with. She was an Acorn legend, and I hope she rests in peace.

Willy, I love you! You definitely were a mama in my heart, and I'm so sad I wasn't around to make it to your funeral because I definitely wanted to share my condolences, not just to you but Nyla as well.

There were so many traumatic events happening at that time. So many people were getting killed left and right. People were making songs glorifying how they were sliding. People really love killing each other down there, and they damn near killed their cousins. It was so sad that half of the young men I went to school with wound up getting killed or going to jail. That's the saddest shit ever. I can't talk about everybody, but people who know about Oakland and know the school I went to should know that I know everything about that and how hectic everything was for everyone. There were definitely a lot of gangs in West Oakland, which is crazy because West Oakland is so small. How could be there be so many different types of gangs? But that was West Oakland. It all started from way back. This phone was from MAC and some original OG West Oakland people. I really wasn't affiliated with a lot of that, but I was forced to be involved because I was in West Oakland. I mean my pride wouldn't let me not beat bitches up for my respect.

Through all the bullshit, I tried to stay positive, and I always remained interested in school, so my grades were never bad until I started going to high school at McClymonds. I transferred to this alternative college prep school called MetWest, which was the best thing that ever happened to me. We had different counselors, teachers, and therapists. We even had a special class for teenagers, which was lucky. Ms. Crystal was counselor. I loved to go to her class because I could get high and yell, but most importantly I could talk to her about what I'd done, and she wouldn't even care. She'd just listen to me and tell me not to get so high, to try to slow down. I love Ms. Crystal because she was very patient, and she took a different approach to other teachers. I had another counselor who really did not connect with me, but I wish she did because she took us on trips and she got us free lunch anytime we had a session with her.

I remember this one boy from Ghost Town, and we had something going on, but he kind of hurt me because he was talking to another girl. It wasn't just the fact he was talking to another girl; it was the fact I'd confided in him about what I was going through with my parents' substance abuse issues, and he told the other girl about my life. When it was time to confront the girl, she had so much to say about me and my struggles, but I had nothing to say about her. I thought the boy I was dating from Ghost Town was more empathetic of my needs and my feelings, but I guess he wasn't. To this day, I still haven't had a conversation with him about that, but I really don't care anymore because I'm healed. At first, I wanted to kill that bitch and beat the fuck out of both of them but later I realized he wasn't in my best interest anyway. He didn't understand my worth to begin with. When I love, I love hard, and that's why people threw salt on my name. They didn't want people to love, and they didn't want me to show them the love I had.

Chapter 5

My mom's Section 8 voucher was running out, and she had to find a place within thirty days. I remember her being so stressed and anxious to look for a place to live. She was so tired of living at my granny's house because she always used to have her own apartment, whether it was a good house or not. She'd been living on her own since she was fifteen years old, so she really wanted to move sooner rather than later. In fact, she wanted to move so soon that we wound up moving to the Lower Bottoms right next to Campbell Village on Chase Street. My mama rented a house from this man named Mr. Benson. She was so grateful he let us stay there, and he was very happy to have us. He said it was his mom's or his grandmother's house and that he lived there since he was a child, and that meant a lot to me.

A lot of people don't know this, but when I moved to Chase Street, the first person I actually met was this French girl. I forgot her name, but she lived right next door to us. She was so sweet, and she spoke three different languages. She was super smart, and she loved to play with me. We talked about so many things, and I really loved the fact she didn't see my color. She saw me for me. I grew apart from her almost instantly unfortunately. Due to her health, her mama never ever let her go outside.

I had another neighbor named Keola, who lived across the street from us. She also went with me to Cole. She had a bunch of brothers and sisters. Keola and I kicked it off really well. Even though we went to school together, she was a little older than me, so we weren't as close at Cole, but when I moved to Chase Street and became neighbors, we got really close really fast. She basically became family. I loved how she had a strong passion for her family just like I did. She also loved music. We used to always have so much fun singing and getting on by impersonating different comedians from TV. At this time, Keola and I first started smoking cigarettes with her sister Meme. I was drunk with them, and I needed to smoke something, but we didn't have any weed, so Keola lit up a cigarette. We were always drunk, and everybody was smoking cigarettes. She explained that people drink because cigarettes and alcohol go hand-in-hand, so I asked to hit the cigarette, and it gave me the heaviest rash I'd ever felt. At the same time, it was so addicting, so that's when I started smoking Newports.

Keola's mama was this lady named Dee. She had this demeanor where you could tell when she opened her mouth, she wasn't to be played with. She really loved her kids and gave them the freedom to be themselves. They could've been going outside all the time, but because they all had a strong bond, they loved to stay in the house and just chill. We would stay in the house after going to Cinépolis, and we'd be chilling, laughing, smoking, and cracking up. We used to really crack each other up so much. Keola was one of my first real friends when I moved to Chase Street. We kicked it off. Even though Keola and I never fought, we definitely got into it, but we respect each other. I also got along with her older sister Meme. We really vibed because I was very mature. Everybody I hung out with was older than me, and a lot of people didn't even know I was as young as twelve when I first moved to West Oakland. I really acted mature, so people often thought I was older. I didn't like telling them how old I actually was because I knew they would look at me as a little girl. They just didn't know how mature my mind was.

When I looked up West Oakland history, I discovered the Harlem Renaissance made it to the neighborhood. There used to be a strip down 7th Street where Bart Street is now that had bars, movies stores, and recording shops. West Oakland is where a lot of the slaves from the South had to migrate for a better life. That is what my granny did, and she ended up working for the Richmond railroad. That's where a lot of black people worked in West Oakland. There are a lot of good waterfront jobs working at the port, but even if you didn't work for the port, there were better opportunities up north with less harsh conditions.

Let me always remind my people that we as black people are still experiencing modern day slavery. The system was designed to sabotage our culture and encourage blacks to kill each other. The system raped our woman and men and stripped them from their family. A lot of people don't know this, but a lot of slave masters raped the hardest African warriors to make his family and tribe look down on his honor. White people did this to make a statement. It was called buck busting. They made us fight and kill each other, they separated us based on our skin tones, and they made us hate our own melanin. We have to remember beating and whipping comes from traumatizing slaves, so they would believe in Christ. Even though Black people didn't put the drugs in places like the projects. It's not a coincidence that there's a liquor store on every corner. And you think those white people fund Planned Parenthood because they care? No, they want to kill black babies. They don't want us to procreate, but we are too strong. If we weren't strong, we would have died off by now.

When you get time, look up Eve's genes. It explains how an African woman is the only woman who can make any color baby. If you don't believe me, you can look even further to the Bible. The Bible refers to this lady who had two babies at the same time. The Bible describes the twins as being total opposites. One baby's hair was curly, and the other's was straight. One baby had blue eyes, and the other baby had brown eyes. I strongly believe this idea because both of my parents are dark brown-skinned, but my baby brother is much lighter. We are they descendants of not just Africans but the French and Indians as well. African Americans are the newest people, including any other third-world places. there are Africans everywhere. Afro-Latinos, Afro-Cubans, Afro-Dominicans, Afro-Haitians, Afro-Jamaicans, Afro-Brazilians. I just want to let people know Africans enslaved themselves as well.

We had a performance coming up, and I was so excited at this point. I needed some brand-new clothes because I was looking like a mess. I knew I had to look presentable, and honestly, I was so tired of looking the way I did. I'd already had it bad enough when Semaj used to say I was a little shit. I remember he made me feel so out of place. When we'd be going somewhere and he didn't like the shoes I had on, he'd start talking shit about me. I really didn't give a fuck, but as soon as he didn't like how I was moving, he clowned on me and told everybody I was wearing his shoes. Like why would you do that? I wouldn't have done anything like that to my best friend. I just didn't have the money at the time, but I had the love, and when we were good, we were the best. Though now that I think about it, he never fought for me. He didn't have to, but I remember I would always support him. Semaj had a strange way of loving. Virgos can be really judgmental and lack awareness. I could have been the same way, but it's not who I am to tell somebody what to wear or how to be. I never put him in a situation where he had to fight someone.

I needed some clothes, so I started stealing. Semaj hooked me up with some bitches, who were going out the way to steal. They ran West Oakland. I was fresh and nobody knew me, so I stole with those bitches often, but got cheated sometimes. I wasn't upset, though, as long as I got some clothes. It was so bad that Semaj's mama was getting notices and letters, but my mama didn't know anything until I got caught with this one bitch who was supposed to be my cousin. I came to find out later that this was the same bitch who made it seem like I left her for dead at my cousin's party when she lived on 66th. Everyone thought I'd stop stealing with those girls after a while because they started being possessive, showing up after school and following home asking Semaj to try to see if I got let out early. I got caught too much, and I knew when a store was hot, and I remember one of the bitches wanted me to go back inside one because she wanted something else. I didn't mind stealing shit, but I wasn't about to go back in and get caught again. She developed an attitude and tried to say some slick shit. I was so mad I snapped on her. I was used to be hella calm, but the bitch kept pressing. I was about to beat her ass because she really had the nerve to try to clown me. I would get her shit, but she could've stolen her own. She immediately shut up after that. She didn't like me after the incident, but I didn't give a fuck because she should've known who she was fucking with. I'd been fighting since I was a child. There were a lot of times bitches were saved just because they were cool with people I was cool with. I respected them, but at the same time, if they pushed me to that point, then that's on them because I gave people too many chances. A lot of bitches respected me, but they didn't like me. They sure didn't say that shit to my face, though, because they wanted me to steal for them. One time, I got caught with this bitch, Precious, at the Davison Street Walmart. It was the same bitch who said I left her at the party on 66th, and she had bitches trying to fight me. They fought the wrong one, though. Right after I beat the girl that Precious tried to stick on me, Precious was nowhere to be found. The group I was with walked all the way from the dead end to Truck's barbershop.

Truck really was overlooked and needs to be acknowledged because of all the people he's seen hurt and how he's had to bury his own people. You have to be special to be able to talk about someone who's deceased without living in the sorrowness of death. This man buried kids, friends, and people very close to him, but when you have a calling, you have to listen to God. You cannot ignore Him.

THE STRUGGLE THAT MADE ME

That bitch got her hair pulled out (fresh singles), and my knuckles were all cut up from her braces. The only bitch who tried to break up the fight was Makira, who was another girl from both East and West Oakland.

Honestly, you can be from a lot of different places. I am from my mom's old coochie. My family is from Sunnyside, but we don't own that street. That is why I'm trying to get people to see this is bigger than just me. I didn't have to mention anyone else. I just know there's a lot of people way more talented than me, and they've been through so much shit that they don't even see the gifts God has given them.

I was so in rage that I almost hit Makira I lost the money I'd just made from selling my little nickel bags. I used to do well selling my bags because none of the dope men knew I sold crack. I had to buy lunch and weed. I wasn't trying to be broke, and I wasn't about to wait on anybody for money, so I would hang out by the 8th, 7th, or 10th Street stores and ask people for a cigarette. I would have the nickel in my mouth while I was talking to them, and then they'd give me the five dollars. I love nickel bags because knocks where knocks, and a lot of the dope men sold solids and dimes, so I did well. A couple of my knocks were classmates who teased me about my mother's appearance, yet their mamas were on the corner looking like Ezale ready to fall into the store. RIP to him, too. I kept a lot of that knowledge to myself because who am I to judge anyone after all the shit I've done? This is why people loved me because I let them be themselves without judgement. I am a Virgo, so people say I should be very judgmental and bossy, but look at Micheal Jackson. There are so many talented people from the Bay. Even Tupac wanted to be from here. He told people when he died, he was from Oakland, but in Oakland, shit is bad enough. There's no longer a sports team here. [Now just the Oakland ass come now you know if they would have had the parade at Lake Merritt they would have been turnt.] There are too many rich people on the other side of the bay in San Francisco. That city has everything, but one thing it's lacking is Oakland's realness

Even though my mom tried to do the best she could, I'd say that wasn't enough in my eyes. Her saying this only made me hate my mom more and more. She made the ugliest face and could barely talk when she was high. I used to hate talking to her about anything when she was in that state. She'd just want to continue fucking with me, so I started fucking with her to throw off her high. I used to know exactly how much she'd smoked by how high she was. Only my brother Major and I knew this about my mom. A lot of people thought she was just drunk a lot, but she really was fucked up. My daddy would be just quiet, but if we fucked up his high, he started whooping our asses. One time, Keshad knocked on the door right after my daddy got high. I don't know why he did that because we all got our asses whooped. Perhaps Keshad didn't care as much because he could more easily get bruises, so my daddy would take it out on me instead, so the teacher wouldn't see. We'd all be put in the corner, and I used to pick at the paint and talk hella shit to myself about myself and my family.

I started branching off in West Oakland from Keola at this time. I was going to school at McClymonds, but McClymonds wasn't the best school for me. However, there was one other girl I kicked it off with. Her name was Maya, and I called her my ride or die because we literally did everything together. I remember having to lie to my mom all the time just to stay out with her. Maya was different just like me. She was a tomboy and, nobody could tell us shit. We respected each other, and I used to hang out with Maya and her cousins from Acorn all the time.

One time we got so drunk, we ended up at my cousin Delana's house, and I threw up all over the bathroom. It was not good, but we had hella fun that night. Even though my cousin Delana was older than me, she still let me have fun and be a teenager. She also told me my life was what I made it. If I wanted to be a bad ass bitch, then that's what I was, but as a Virgo, she also knew I was a hustler and that I was going to get whatever I said I wanted—just like she did. I looked up to my older cousin in a lot of ways because she didn't let anything get to her. She always broke her mind and she always looked good. I was mature for my age, so sometimes she would have a hard time remembering how old I was. She'd forget to tell me "no" if I wanted to do certain things when I was in her house, which I really respected, but at the same time I was going to do what I wanted regardless.

Just like Major, I was working at the Highland Hospital Modern Neighborhood Program, where Major had done an internship. My brother wanted to be a radiologist, and I thought that was so cool he wanted to be a doctor who deals with X-rays. I loved the Neighborhood Modern Program, it just wasn't for me with all of the blood and tools we had to use, but I graduated to get my 500-dollar stipend. After I graduated, I went to work with Bill again, but when I got too old to work for him, I started stealing and selling drugs.

My older brother Greg was in and out of jail, but he was back home at this point when he met a lady name Roslyn who lived in Campbell Village. They loved each other, but their relationship was definitely toxic, and there was a lot of drama back and forth. My brother wound up going to jail for domestic violence and has been there ever since 2013. My brother definitely was not in his right mind at the time he went to jail, but he was old enough to make his own decisions. I really hope this time around when he comes home, he'll do right because life is too short, and we value family. There also was a little drama between Greg's girlfriend's daughter, Keola, and me. It kind of messed up Greg's and my relationship, but at the same time, he'd never lose my family, so it was never serious enough to hurt our friendship. After Keylow, who was Keola's brother died, we grew apart. I really loved Keylow. We were the same age, and Greg couldn't stand us because I felt like he was sick of the girl drama going on between us. He was a solid person like a real standup guy. There are not too many people out there willing to ride for their family or people they love. I took his death very hard. He was the first person to pass away who I was close besides Shanika. My mom tried her best to be there for the family by sending love and prayers and sometimes making them food for comfort. They were really going through it as a family. I saw them mourn. It's so sad when a family goes through something so horrific.

Chapter 6

Time passed and as I got a little older, I started rapping and writing music and my grades started dropping, so my mom and dad decided to put me in a school called MetWest, which is a college prep school in Oakland. It's internship based, and I did not want to transfer at all initially. I really liked where I was even though my grades were dropping a little bit, so I felt that I needed just a little time to redeem myself so I could continue to go to McClymonds, but my mom or dad weren't having it. I remember the conversation we had about transferring. I was with my younger friend Trisha, and I was throwing a tantrum because I didn't want to go MetWest, but it was the best thing to ever happen to me. It was the first time I could really be creative and explore things that I like, although I hated the fact that if we weren't on time with our homework, it didn't count. That pissed me off because I would work extra hard just to make sure my homework was on point, and sometimes it would be only four or five minutes late. Black people are never on time, however, that motivated me to get up early and try to be there before school started. I guess that's one of the reasons I became my own boss because I'm never on time.

When I first arrived at MetWest, I was very shy because I didn't know anybody except my cousin Janessa. Janessa was biracial, and she was a little dinky. I loved my cousin because she accepted me for me, and she pushed me to do better, even though we were in two different grades and in different advisories. She would always come check on me, but she knew I was hella smart. She didn't want me to get into it with anybody, but when it came down to protecting her, I was quick to defend. She also wasn't from the Bay Area, so I was very overprotective of her due to the simple fact she wasn't a fighter and she basically could get taken advantage of, but she was older than me, and she could stand her ground, especially when it came down to her little boyfriend she used to have in high school. I loved Nessa. I remember going to her house all the time from school and just chilling with her and her mom or smoking with her boyfriend. We'd always be cracking up and having a good time. She also had a little brother named Reggie who played the PlayStation with my little brothers all the time. They used to be so funny when they'd argue over whose turn it was to play.

I also became very close to this boy named Quindale. He was my peer coach, who were other students who helped you with anything you had going on in school. My peer coach Quindale was a clown. He was the only one who could really put me on my back cracking up. I loved my peer coach, however he used to give up on his work all the time. I used to try to push him, but sometimes I was going through so much, and I really couldn't help him like I needed to.

That summer was one of the last times I worked for Bill. I remember I won a bonus, and I came in the house and threw all of the money around the living room. I was so happy I could get some new clothes and go places all summer. That night, I picked up all of my money and hid it under my bed thinking no one was going to get it, but I woke up to my mom under my bed stealing it. I asked her why she was in my room, and she said she needed some help and that she'd pay me back later. I told her that I was tired of her stealing my money, and she said it'd be the last time. She wouldn't do it anymore, but in that moment, she really needed it. I was so fed up with her that I just gave her the money, which came to about fifty dollars. I went back to sleep until I woke up again to my dad asking me for another twenty dollars. I was so fed up with both of them. I'd been fed up for years, but when I started making my own money and started to understand they were taking what I'd worked hard for, I got getting madder and madder. I started being more disrespectful every time they got sober to remind them how much I hated that wishy-washy shit. Every time they were sober, they wanted to act like parents and punish me, but when they were high, they would take my money but let me do whatever I wanted to do. It was so fucked up. They used to get crack from our neighbor next door, and I hated it because they would wait a long time to pay her back, and then she would talk shit. It was just chaos. I never understood why she would give them some crack knowing they'd already borrowed some crack from you. It was stupid.

On top of all of this, my mom thought just because nobody cooperated, she could ask anybody for something and not have to pay them when she was supposed to or when she told people she would. I hate people like that. Don't tell me you're going to give me something back and then when I ask for it, get an attitude. My mama was that type of crackhead, and that hurt my soul because she'd often ask for things knowing she didn't have the money to pay. I knew every dealer my mom and dad used from East Oakland to West Oakland.

Everyone. At the end of the day, my parents were the type of people who liked buying from the people with the good shit. If the shit was bad, they'd moving on to the next person and deal with them for a minute.

Back at school, I hated the fact I worked so hard and was barely rewarded for anything. A lot of people knew I was smart and always told me keep up the good work, but they didn't know the hard time I was having. I wouldn't even eat breakfast most mornings because my mom and dad were too lazy to get up and fix my brothers and me something to eat. Often that was when they'd just have come down from their high. I used to hate asking people for food. My mom used to tell me she'd come by the school to bring me lunch, but most of those time I went hungry or had to eat the nasty cafeteria food. My mom knew she was out of pocket because when I asked for some lunch money, she wouldn't have a dollar to her name. She'd have to call around or if my Major was around, she'd ask him, but people hated giving my mom money because they knew she'd get high all night and not have a dollar the next morning. I made a lot of promises to myself after seeing what to do and what not to do.

Everyone respected my mom because she had a good heart, but a lot of people never witnessed the evil I experienced due to her being sick. I'd watch my mom get up to start her day. She said she was doing the best she could, but every night she'd always find a way to get high on crack, smoke a whole pack of cigarettes, and have a pint of gin or whatever my parents were drinking for the night. When I started calculating all the money she was spending on that bullshit, I was disappointed she couldn't give us a good breakfast. All the while, she wanted me to well good in school. I hated the thought of my mom and dad putting drugs before me. I started speaking my mind. I got my ass whooped every time, but that just made me angrier. I would always go out my way to make everyone happy, but I felt like nobody ever went out their way for me. I never got anything I really wanted, especially as the only girl with five brothers. Everyone thought I was spoiled until they hung around long enough to see exactly why I acted the way I did.

My mom worked nine-to-five jobs while my dad recycled. My mom didn't get on welfare until later. For a long time, a lot of people didn't know my mom wasn't on welfare. She was working low class jobs, which didn't do much because she and my dad were addicted to crack. I never had my own room until we moved to the Muslim house on 61st, but even then, my dad rented half of my room out, so I never had my own privacy. I finally had my own room on Chase Street for a couple of years before my mom let an old friend come stay with us. He had cancer and wound up dying in my room. Now why would I want to go back into a room that had had a dead man in it?

At one point, I really hated my life, and I didn't have anybody who truly had my back. Even the people I called my close friends didn't know what was going through. Because I got teased so much when I was younger about my parents being on drugs, I never wanted to talk about it with people. But the thing about West Oakland is everybody's mamas were up to something: gambling, getting high, hoeing, stealing, scamming. But I still felt that we were better. Once you're in West Oakland, it's so hard to get out. Not only is it hard to get out, it's dangerous. It's the targeted area intended to destroy the black community. Rich people would privately fund Planned Parenthood because it was away to kill the black community off. My mom let her kids move to West Oakland after she'd had a hard battle with leaving. She was in and out of programs trying to get clean. At the time we moved, she said she didn't have a choice and that we would move soon. She knew something was bound to happen with our being in West Oakland. It was only a matter of time. Nobody can shine down there because there's so much fake shit. The realest people from West Oakland were facing life sentences or buried six feet under.

Despite all the bullshit I was going through, I met some real bitches and met some fake ones too. I used writing as an outlet for whenever I wanted to beat somebody's ass or kill myself because I didn't want to go through what was troubling me. Writing made me feel so much better. I could write damn near all night. I remembered every time I was punished I would write raps and draw. At this point, I was just starting at MetWest and trying to figure out what internship I wanted to pursue. I loved that MetWest would let us pick where we wanted to intern. I was at MetWest for a couple of years, and I did a lot of things pertaining to my African roots like making waist beads with a woman who was an African dance teacher. I also took a class on how to treat African hair and what vitamins to use for black hair. I loved the fact that MetWest was place where I could be myself. It was very unlike McClymonds where people thought I was weird because I loved doing my work before skipping school. My ride or die, Maya, used to know that I was ready right after I turned in my papers. I missed her the most when I transferred. That was one bitch that really loved me for me, and she never tried to for me to change. She respected everything about me.

Chapter 7

As I started getting older, I started to fall out with my parents. It was hard for me to listen to someone who took money from their own kids and only thought about alcohol and crack. It also hurt me a lot that they'd put on such a front for people. Everybody thought they were decent parents despite us looking kind of dirty. Some people never even knew my mom smoked crack, which really irritated my soul because I'd seen her at her lowest.

During the summer before my tenth-grade year at MetWest, I found a science program near our house in West Oakland. It was on the best streets near 14th, and nobody really knew about the program. It was a paid stipend program of about 500 dollars. It included a six-week course, so I thought it would be perfect for my little brother and me, especially since we both liked science. Ray Ray liked science even more than me, so I thought he'd find it very interesting for both of us to do. The summer program had machines that calculated the particulate matter in the air. We studied the environment in West Oakland and in Berkeley and discovered that Berkeley's air was about five times cleaner than in West Oakland due to the port and the diesel trucks in the area. The fact is most projects or ghettos are by places that are populated with particulate matter or heavy exhaust leading people to develop cancer, asthma, and other lung diseases. It's very disappointing.

We had two instructors at the science program: a lady named Sandra and a man named David. Sandra was a black, heavyset lady. She was short and cute. David was a regular white guy with glasses. I really appreciated both of them for sharing their time to teach us about the environment and show us what causes the air to be more or less polluted with particular matter.

At this time, Ray Ray was about twelve or thirteen, and I was fifteen turning sixteen. To get to the science program, Ray Ray and I used to walk just a couple of blocks from our house, but on this particular day Ray Ray went off with his friends early in the morning and showed up late to the program. Ray Ray's eyes were bloodshot, and when I saw him, I knew he was high. Instantly, I was so embarrassed and so mad at him at the same time, but I really couldn't get that mad because I was popping pills, smoking weed, and doing shit I didn't have any business doing. I never smoked with my little brother, and I never wanted him to use drugs. They take over your body, but I knew he was going to get a hold of them somehow one day. We were in West Oakland after all. I couldn't be too mad at him. I just told him to watch who he did drugs with and to be very careful. After that I started smoking with him just because I knew he was going to do it anyway. At the program, we had snacks, and he went to the snack bar about three times. He didn't even like sun chips, and he was eating the hell out of those. I just remember telling him to go wash his face and his hands and to straighten up because I didn't know how David or Sandra would discipline him if they knew he was high. I smoked every day, so my tolerance was high, and nobody really noticed if I'd been smoking.

That summer was wild. We went to every party in West Oakland, and sometimes we even went to the functions downtown. I really didn't like going to a party with a lot of people, but sometimes I took Ray Ray with me. He usually wanted to go because he was already experiencing little house parties, but those weren't as wild as the house parties I went to. Initially, I was hesitant to bring my little brother because at the time I was popping pills and was reckless, but when I was with him, I made sure every move was worth it. I also liked showing him the ropes and what life was really about or what I wanted to believe it was about at the time. As an older sibling, I wanted to take responsibility for the examples I showed my younger brothers. Even though Ray Ray and I were close in age, I was a little more mature than him, so I could be around eighteen-year-olds without issue, but when I was with him, I went to younger parties.

I remember going to like four parties with my little brother, but one time I told my daddy we were going to a party when I really just wanted to go to Ghost Town to beat this little bitch up for talking smack to me on the Internet. This was back when Myspace and MocoSpace first came out, and at the time, I had a friend named Dontell who I was really close with, but Dontell fucked with bitches I knew to be popular. Some knew of me; some didn't. I knew a lot of people from East, West, and North Oakland. Dontell and I had a falling out over a little girl who supposedly took my little boyfriend who I'd confided in about my mom's addiction and my living situation, so I really wasn't feeling bad, but he apologized, and I forgave him. However, I never forgot how bad he hurt me. Dontell made up for it by allowing me to fight the girl, and I beat the fuck out of her friend because her friend wouldn't let me fight her. She wanted to be Captain Save-a-Hoe, and got her ass beat. I feel so bad because I had my little brother and his partner Maria with me, and on top of that, we were in Ghost Town. I drew a lot of attention to us. We were on 27th and Sycamore Street, and that bitch thought I was playing. All I remember is her head hit on a gate hella fast, and I grabbed her and dropped her. I let her get up and then took off from her again. One of the bitches she was with had gone to school with me in East Oakland, and I'm surprise she didn't tell her friend about me before the fight. I'd made a name for myself in East Oakland, and now I had to make a name for myself in West Oakland. The police came shortly after, but we were gone by then. I had to start from scratch when we moved, which was okay because I didn't want everybody to know I knew how to fight that well. I only fought when I needed to, but in West Oakland you have to fight to the death. It's either a win, a loss, or a draw, and I wasn't going out regardless.

From that day forward, Dontell and I kept a good friendship regardless of where we were at or who we were with. We always acknowledged each other. Dontell has been through so much after losing his brother to the gang Affiliation. Most of our older brothers and sisters were in that gang. If that wasn't the case, they were in Stubby or P-Team or Dipset. It was like living in a movie. Everybody knew someone who'd died. When you live in that type of environment, it's like living in a war zone. You're often so scared not knowing what's about to happen at any given moment, and West Oakland is much smaller than East Oakland, so everything and everyone is super close, including the enemies. It was so exciting but at the same time scary. You couldn't trust anybody. In fact, a lot of people thought trust was a weakness, and that's an area where I felt people wanted to test me even more.

There was an outreach program for kids called The Center right on 8th and Willow. When we first moved down to Chase Street, I used to walk right past it. It took me a couple summers to finally venture in and explore inside. I always saw bad ass kids in front play fighting and cussing. My little brother went there before me to play basketball. He also went to the Discover Center on Cypress right across the street from Cole. At Discover Center, my brother became familiar with an afterschool tutor by the name of Howard Nathel or "Batman," which is what my son calls him now. Howard was now a retired scientist who did a lot of outreach work for the kids in the community. We'd met him at the rec center in Campbell Village, and since then he'd been close with our family. He and Mo Campbell assisted with Keshad's first flag football and basketball teams. They provided support and paid fees, but also had my little brother running trails and jogging up hills. Howard even had Keshad running marathons. He called Keshad a knucklehead head whenever Keshad needed to straighten up his act. I think he saw something very special in Keshad. He also developed a close relationship with this man named Shondrel, who had a son named Nichols. He and Keshad were close and played basketball and hung out.

One day, Keshad got an ass beating so bad because a girl said he'd put a hickey on her neck. When I heard what he'd gotten a whooping for, I thought maybe he hadn't done it. I knew he was sneaky, but giving girls hickies didn't sound like him. Either way, my dad left big bruises on him that time. Keshad was the lighted child. Everyone else is dark skinned, which doesn't blow my mind because our ancestors were raped, so those genes are still in us, and they can pop out at any generation. Also, being Black Americans, we're mixed with native blood from natives who were already in the Americas.

Chapter 8

I remember walking home from school one day, and this badass little girl named Barbra asked me what my name was and where I was from. At first, I just laughed it off and started walking toward my house, but the little girl started following and taunting me. She was with another girl named Sacarri. I gave these little bitches a bunch of chances to stop fucking with me, but I finally got mad enough to get in their faces. I told them to go get someone for me to fight, and I was serious about it. I didn't want to fight anybody, but I knew if I sent those little girls back home bloodied, somebody was going to be at my door, so I told them to get their big sister. I experienced a lot of situations like this. The little girl never got her sister, but I often imagine how many fights I could've been in just based on this one small altercation. It really wasn't shit to me, but it could have been. The little girls and I were cool later on, and was a reason why it didn't escalate. I'm happy I didn't have to fight her auntie or cousin because it would have gone down. At this time, nobody really knew me yet, but I was getting around silently and quickly. I noticed everyone who'd seen me fight had a lot more respect for me, but I didn't like that because I felt people wanted to see me brake. But I was still standing. I was wild. My friends and I used to go on knock out missions and rob people by the Bart. I used to pop them Bart Simpsons and be at the West Oakland Bart station trying to come up with a Homer. It was our joke, but I hope all those people forgive me. I was going through a lot, and really didn't mean to harm anyone.

Semaj was my closest friend at the time, and I would go everywhere with him around the Bottoms. We already had a rapping group and were doing well, and we used to crack up talking about people, including ourselves. Semaj knew everyone because he was related to almost everyone. Semaj's older cousin Shawana worked at the middle school we were going to, and I began to notice he wasn't trying to get sent to the office as often. I loved Shawana. She was a pleasant spirit, and she was always dressed well and treated people with respect, but when it came to her family, she had a whole other side. We went on a field trip to the San Francisco Zoo one day, and I became super hungry. I didn't have any money, so I stole a cheeseburger. Shawana tried to prevent me from getting in trouble by paying for the cheeseburger herself, but they still kicked the whole school out the zoo because I'd stolen the cheeseburger. I was sad, but I wasn't embarrassed. I couldn't go on any more field trips after that because they banned me.

One day, I branched off from Semaj and ran into these two bitches with yarn locs. One was a tall, light-skinned girl, and the other was a short, brown-skinned girl. The tall one had these pretty gold and black yarn braids, and the short girl had some black and burgundy yarn locs. I'd seen them at cypress store rolling a blunt before, so I asked who'd done their hair, and the short one responded, "I did." Her name was Tatiana, but people called her Tati. The other girl's name was Mazionna. I met them again in a different predicament, Mazi was rapping. I'd seen a couple of bitches rap, but I'd never met anybody who could rap like Mazionna. When I say this bitch got gas, I mean for the first time, I found a real bitch I could relate to. We popped it off when we started rapping back and forth, and then we really popped it off when we found out we were both Virgos. I love Virgos even though we clash at times, but Mazionna and I never fought. We definitely play fought, but that was a sign of respect. We'd lose or draw, we both weren't ever going out. Mazionna beat the fuck out of bitches. She was a Campbell Village Original, CVG, a real West Oakland bitch who earned her stripes with blood, sweat, and tears. Most of Tati's family was from 96th in the Alphabets. I'd seen both of them around, but this was my first time actually meeting them. They went to Fremont together but wound up going to different schools the next year, which made me really close with Tati because the school she went to was right by MetWest.

I started hanging out with Mazi and Tati all the time after school. It became a routine. Mazi and I would branch off from Tati and go to the studio. There was a lot of talent in West Oakland. Often people struggling the most are the most talented. I remember Mazi and I ran into a man named Mike Mike. Mike Mike was so talented, he could play a beat on his chest and still rap to the song. There are crack heads down there who can sing better than Whitney Houston, no lie. When I noticed how talented Mazi was, I wanted to motivate her to get better and be a star. We fed off of each other and were the girl version of Lil Boosie and Webbie—real savages. When we were together, nobody—and I mean nobody—could fuck with us. We weren't scared to stand up for ourselves. Mazi was hotheaded, and a lot of people didn't understand her, but I did. I understood and respected her goals, and that's why I really think we never fought each other. We both respected each other. My heart was always pure, and I think real recognized real.

We had so many fights in the Bottoms. Mazi had way more fights than me, but I remember this one particular fight she had with a scary ass bitch. I was not present during this fight; however, I know what happened. Mazi fucked that girl up. The girl was so scared, the next fight they had, she picked up a crowbar and hit Mazi on her top lip, slitting her whole lip open. Now if that isn't a coward move, I don't know what is. The fact that she could spit on someone while that person's holding a baby but then couldn't take an ass whooping is crazy to me. The girl even would come over Tati's house sometimes to try to make us feel bad because the bitch couldn't go outside without knowing where Mazi was. This is the same bitch that carried a pistol. I've seen bitches so scared they can't go anywhere without a weapon or someone to help them. And that's what really gets me about West Oakland: the legends die or go to jail because of people who are so scared they will literally back door their own family to be in streets. It really opened my eyes to what was going on around me. The weakest people would pray on the strongest to get them out the way, and it worked every time because the weak would let their ego and pride take over.

I understood I didn't have anything to prove, but if you fucked with me enough I was going to show you exactly who you were fucking with, but that's what I was afraid of. It was too easy to die or go to jail, too easy to fight and slide on shit. I wanted to be more, and I wanted to but show people how special we really are.

Tati had two older sisters Meme and Nika. I didn't see Meme too much because she was always in East Oakland, but sometimes she came to her granny's, who lived at the end of Campbell Village. It was always turned up when Meme came. From weed to pills to alcohol, we always got high when she was around. I knew when Meme visited, I was going to get drunk as fuck. I remember the first time I got drunk was with Tati, Meme, and Nika. I got so drunk I had to go to the bathroom and throw up. I was in the bathroom for about thirty minutes before we walked to the store. As we started down the street, I became dizzy and I ran into a pole. I had the biggest knot on my forehead. It wasn't even funny. I sobered up real fast after that because those bitches couldn't stop laughing at me. They laughed the whole walk home.

At the time, Nika was dating an older man, and he took care of Nika very well. Whatever Nika wanted, she got, but I see why he chose Nika to be his girl. She was very nurturing and loving, and when it came to him, she would always be empathetic to his needs. She made sure his food was ready, ran any errands for him, and also took care of his daughter, who was about three years old. Nika was so beautiful with long, thick hair. She had a caramel complexion and had a nice shape to her. A lot of men liked Nika in the hood, but she was too loyal to be taken that easy. Guys already knew not to talk to her because her man would come after them or she was gone turn them down. I would go to stay at Nika's house every day after school.

When I was around thirteen years old, I remember telling everyone I was fifteen when my birthday rolled around. Some people believed me, but others knew I was way younger than the other kids I hung out with. Mama Gina, Tati's mama, called me out so cold. I couldn't lie to her. Mama Gina was very understanding, and I could talk to her about a lot of stuff. She saw what I was going through and how I was handling my business. She said as long as I stayed in school, she couldn't say shit.

I would be punished a lot for not calling my parents. I would have to call home every hour when I was away, and I hated that. Sometimes when I would call my mom, I would hear how she was, so I would stop calling her thinking she wasn't thinking about me, but when she came down from her high, you best believe she was calling Tati, Meme, Semaj, and Mama Gina looking for Poodie. I hated that shit because I tried to communicate as best as I could, but I couldn't tell if my mama knew I was having too much fun. I didn't want my parents to cut my fun off just to sit in my house while they were getting high and having their own fun all night.

Chapter 9

At this age, I was definitely understanding life on a different level, and I started to see people for who they were and not what they were wearing. Even a bum could be worth more than gold, so I observed people's character and how they moved with or without people. I started realizing a lot of people were just trying to impress those they thought were more important. They also treated people they thought were beneath them like step kids. No matter what I heard about someone, I always gave them a chance to show me who they were. A lot of people liked that I gave them a chance and didn't burn their bridges, But there were a lot of hoes who tried to play. When it came to helping people, I didn't mind, but as I started going through things personally, I realized that I only had myself at the end of the day. Even with five brothers, I never ran to anyone about my problems. There were a lot of reasons why I didn't call my brothers when shit got rough. One of the main reasons was because my brothers always thought I was the problem because of how rebellious and stubborn I was at times, but I was only that way because they made me that way. When I was out in public or at school, I wouldn't say I was an angel, but I was a little more shy. Also, I understood things can go left really fast, and I didn't want to put my brothers into any situations that they weren't trying to put themselves in. I held my own. There were a lot of people telling my older brother about me when he came back home from jail. I was happy but at the same time I was terrified for all my brothers but mostly Major. His name spoke for itself, and you felt his presence anytime he came into the room but not because he wanted attention. It was just something he gave off from the time he was born. To me, he was just my big-headed brother, who was with the shit and wanted to show off all the time. When he came home, I remember us watching black hood movies like *Menace to Society*, *Belly*, *Blue Street Avenue*, *Juice*, *Friday*, *Don't Be a Menace*, and other movies. He really enjoyed laughing and roasting others. He was roasted often enough to be the super roaster because he could make you cry, and if he saw you getting mad, he would make it worse. I used to be in my feelings until I started roasting his ass back, and at that point I knew a lot of personal things, so I tried to get him where it hurt every time. I could tell when it worked because he would roast me less and less. I started having roasts ready for him soon as he walked in the house. At this point, Major's and my relationship started improving even though we would still argue, but we had one of our last fights in West Oakland. I can't remember exactly why we started fighting, but I believe I was trying to go with Mazionna to the studio when my brother tried to check me about something. Of course, I couldn't keep my mouth closed. Sometimes it was better for me to just shut up, especially with my older brother. He didn't make an example out of me too bad because, honestly, he'd beaten my ass way worse before, but the fact it was in front of everybody made a statement. He even yelled out, "This my lil' sister! I can do whateva I need to do to her. She gon' respect me every time."

I hated him and didn't talk to him for some months after that, and all the boys didn't talk to me because they knew Major was my brother. Some guys didn't give a fuck and still tried. I was a virgin at this point, and even though a lot of people thought I was really fast, I was not fucking. I remember Major saw me cozied up with some boy, and he scared the shit out of that poor kid. The boy didn't even want to look my way afterward.

At this time, Major was with his first baby mama, Audrianna. They were so in love, and even had my niece Amajah out of love. I thought they would have lasted a long time, and they did, but as Major got more involved in West Oakland, it started to take a toll on their relationship. Every relationship has two sides to every story, from my perspective, Major really tried to be a loyal man and good father, but yet again West Oakland will eat men up and spit them out. My brother took the name of a man who ran West Oakland at one point in time, and because of that Major was a legacy. My brother encouraged me to stay out of trouble and not be fast. That kind of made me curious about what was out there in West Oakland. I would go to parts of Ghost Town, Acorn, Dog Town, Cypress, and the Bottoms. I would also head downtown and to parties in the east. I used to love to go to parties in the east even though it was hella dangerous. I remember we all went to a party on 88th in Hillside. There were a lot of young Acorn bitches, and I knew they knew who they were. I felt like they really didn't like me, but they didn't have any other choice than to respect me. I'd lived in the Acorn High Rises before hanging out in the Bottoms, and I swam in the Acorn project's pool before I moved to Campbell Village so, a lot of these girls knew of me, and some had even seen me fight.

THE STRUGGLE THAT MADE ME

They really respected me when I ran into my cousin Natalia. Whenever we would see each other, I swear it felt like Arroyo, our old day care. She was with all the bitches who I went to Elmhurst or Webster with. On this particular night, the Acorn girls and I were outnumbered, so I thanked God I was from East Oakland because if I had been from West Oakland that day, it would have been a wrap for everyone I was with.

I am glad I already had a name before moving to West Oakland, and my name was definitely valid. It became more valid because I started moving real mean. My mom and dad were still really bad smokers at this point. It was sad because most of the time, we had to fight for ourselves. Major did have a job, but after that he started hustling and grinding again. He actually started working at the store and doing business with the Muslims. When I was down there, I noticed Major was the only person the Muslim trusted. I don't know how Major won over their trust, but that was some boss shit. At this time, he started hanging out with Marcus. The original Bottom boys were Marcus and Hoodie Boodie. Both of them unfortunately died due to gang violence. Boodie died first, and Marcus was killed about five years afterward. These men weren't another statistic to me; they were family from East Oakland to East Oakland. I can count about sixty people younger than my brother and me who were lost through the years. If I close my eyes, I can still see their smiles and hear their voices.

My mom finally started working at the 99 Cent story in West Oakland. This was the first job she'd had since we'd moved. My dad was working at the Marriott, however, we still struggled due to their addiction. This is one of the reasons we always had someone living with us. That made it easier for them to get high, but they would still always be broke, so I don't know if it really helped, but I do know I was used to people staying with us while it made it hard for my older brother to be comfortable. When I wasn't in punishment, I would go to Keola's house always. Keola's older sister kind of fell out with for whatever reason, which made me feel like they didn't want me to be around, even though Keola and I never really fell out. Keola is really like the big sister I never had. I even felt I had to prove myself to her and the whole of West Oakland. You see, I was never a shit starter, and I was hella small when I was younger. I was really skinny, maybe only 135 pounds. There was a time Keola and I agreed to make up, but it never got past that.

Chapter 10

One day, as I was out in the early morning, I saw this skinny, Chihuahua looking bitch, who fucked everybody's man around the hood, walking down the street. It so happened that Tati had some unfinished beef with her. We'd seen her in the 9th Street store, and Tati must have slapped the dog shit out of her. The girl was saying so much shit, telling Tati she was going to go get her sister and that she didn't care. At the same time as Tati slapped her, another girl come out of the store, and she immediately started choking the hoe, shouting, "Bitch, you fucked my boyfriend!"

At this point, it was entertaining. The store's clerk was trying to break the fight up, and my dumb ass got caught stealing some candy. That man was so mad, he kicked everybody out of the store because he thought we were trying to set him up. That wasn't my intention, but then I realized I didn't have any lunch for school so I tried to get what I could. As we walked off and parted ways, the bitch made sure she let us know she was going to call all her sisters and cousins. I didn't think anything of it because it wasn't my beef. It was all shit I had nothing to do with. That day I got my phone taken in class, and when I got my phone back at the end of the day, I had so many missed calls and text messages. I couldn't even check all of them before Tati started calling me. I was at the bus stop when she told me the bitch brought her fat ass cousin to fight me. I was in shock, honestly. I instantly became furious. Why do bitches always want to fight me when I didn't do shit? She was just looking for a reason, so that day she got it. I told Tati not to trip. I would be on my way. She warned me they were deep and told me if I needed Nika's man to come get me from the Bart, he would. I told her I was ready for whatever. At this point, I wonder why Tati and the bitch weren't fighting again, but I suddenly got a call from Semaj's older cousin. who was now in West Oakland. This was the first time she's called me other than to get a hit, so I felt a lot of pressure to go to West Oakland. I felt like people wanted to see a fight, and thought I was scary. This made me even more ready to tear a patch out of someone. I was tired of bitches coming for me. I got on the 62 bus, which ran all the way down 7th Street, and on this bus, my mom called me and told me there was a gang of bitches down the street and that she would meet me in the village where Tati lived. I assured everyone that I was coming. I was so humble, but deep down inside I wanted to kill. I couldn't stop thinking of the fact that bitches were looking for little ol' me. I got off the bus, and I heard someone say, "Poodie, get in." It was Nika with her man. They drove us to Tati's house where I waited for my parents.

My parents were older, so they didn't like all of the chaos, so they got straight to the point. My mom asked who wanted to fight me. Tati said the girls had left, and they went to my house, so I told my mom and dad I was about to fight the fat girl because Tati had slapped her cousin. My mom asked why Tati wasn't going to fight her, and Tati explained they had all come over, but the chihuahua-looking bitch didn't want to fight Tati again, and the big, fat bitches wanted to fight me. My mom and dad did not want me to fight, but I explained to them that if I didn't fight her now, they would jump the shit out of me, so I called Semaj's cousin back and told her if she wanted to fight, to meet me at my house. It was only my parents and me who walked from the village to my house, but as soon as we got to the middle of Chase Street, I saw about three cars pull up. A lot of bitches bounced out, but the bitch who wanted me was extra big and mean for some reason. At first my dad and mom tried to talk to them as adults, but we instantly started fighting. All of a sudden, it seemed like everybody from the neighborhood was outside. I started uppercutting, ducking through combos. I even had her on the ground for a minute until her family broke it up, but even then, I didn't care how much bigger she was. We went for two rounds, and if it were up to me, I would have tried to fight her until I saw her take her last breath. She was a good challenge, but I got the best of her. The ass whooping I gave her she deserved. That's what you get for trying to pick a fight with someone that hadn't done shit. I honestly felt it wasn't my fight to begin with, but I wanted to show her that was the last time she was going to be able to bully me. Semaj was there. Mazionna was there. I remember a lot of people from the Bottoms showed up, but I mostly remember Semaj's family being there, and I don't know if they wanted to see me fight or be messy, but it didn't matter. I had to do what I had to do.

After the fight, Keola knocked on my door with some basketball shorts and sneakers wanting to know if I was okay. I loved her even if she didn't jump in or wasn't there to help me fight. The fact she checked on me was sweet. I was nauseous after the fight, not because I was a scared, but because I wanted to kick that girl's ass even harder. I let her have it, but I wasn't thinking when I was fighting. I was just mad. Before the second round, my daddy wanted me to get me form together and throw some punches correctly like he thought me. He wanted me to jab and hit her with my more powerful hand, but honestly, I wanted to do more than just box that bitch. I wanted to kill her with my bare hands. She is so lucky I was still respectful after that ass whooping because I wanted to bully her every time I saw her after that just to show her how that shit feels, but that actually wasn't the last time I had a problem with her. After the fight, I threw up because my nerves were so bad. I called Semaj's cousin and asked who'd won. I told her to tell the bitch I wanted to go a for a third round. I was that pissed off. She didn't do too much to me, but I had these long scratch mark that showed the white meat of my skin. I remember my daddy using alcohol all over my neck, and that shit burned like a bitch, but my adrenaline was still rushing.

Keola later told me that the Chihuahua-looking bitch was mad after I beat up her fat ass cousin, who turned skinny after I beat her ass. She started running her mouth to Keola about how I think I am so hard. She said she couldn't wait for somebody to get on me. She said I was going to get what I got coming. She hated how I thought I was the shit, but when I heard all of this, I wasn't surprised. I was more confused by how that bitch thought she could run her mouth about a solid person to another solid person. Of course, Keola was going to tell me everything this bitch said. She was an outsider as far as I was concerned. Keola was very, very special to me, and when her brother Keylow passed away, I gained a love that was beyond friendship. Even before Keylow died, she was a person I could vent to whenever I wanted to get away from home. I really appreciated the Colston family. They have overcome a lot, and through it all, they manage to stay together and hold on to their family. And that is what Keola and I had. We both had a lot of siblings, and both of our parents experienced drug addiction. Also, her dad's name was Kenny and my dad's name was Kenny.

At this point, I fucked with who I fucked with. That was Tati, Nika, Keola, Mazi, Portia and Mimi, Bev Pooh sometimes, Jayana, Makira, the twins, and Jo-Jo. Those were the people I was caught with the most. I was already betrayed by Precious, who was supposed to be my cousin. That was one of the first fights I had in the Bottoms because Precious told everyone I'd left her at a party in East Oakland. Precious and my relationship was never the same after that, and

I felt I was the bigger person due to what I knew I could do to her. I also felt she tried to betray my character. I told her to come on too many times before I left. Whether she remembers or not, I felt she wanted to watch me get my ass beaten when she should have been fighting her own battles.

One day, Nika was on the 40L bus talking to me on the phone. I was about to get out of school, and she was on her way to meet me coming from the east. All of a sudden, Rachelle, one of the twins from the Bottoms, and the Chihuahua-looking bitch got on the same bus as Nika. Nika was by herself, so I stayed on the phone with her. As soon as the bitch saw Nika, she started talking shit about her. Then she repeated what she said about me, how I was eventually going to get beaten up because I thought I was hard. The whole time the girl's talking shit, I am sprinting to the bus, so I can hop on. It definitely was some karma of the highest level because Nika didn't say one word to the bitch. She just kept telling me what stop she was at, so I would know how close they actually were. I was on 5th Avenue and International when I saw the bus about two blocks away. I almost missed it. I had already beaten her cousin's ass, so now it was time to shut this bitch up once and for all.

I don't think this bitch had ever gotten her ass beaten like I did that day. I've beaten a lot of bitches up, but I went into a rage. I was banging her head from seat to seat, punching her face all the while. I aimed at every piercing I saw and was just about to rip out her cheap Tasha pack weave she'd just bought. The twin looked like she was in total shock. She didn't know I was coming. Shit, even I didn't know I was coming. I had to let her know why I was giving her the ass kicking because I was never a bully in West Oakland, but I handled my own. Honestly, there were probably lot of bitches who felt they had the leg up over me, but I later revealed it's not about being the hardest bitch. It's about respect, and if you pushed me far enough, I would handle what needed to be handled. I gave out extra chances just so I wouldn't have to be the bad guy. I was tired of bitches fucking with me.

After I'd fought her fat cousin, why did she want to keep gossiping? Like I wouldn't dog walk this bitch... As I got on the bus, I looked all the way to the back and saw Nika smiling hella hard at me. Nika had a poker face. She could be mad as fuck with a grin on her face. That's just how she was. She never held grudges for too long or was upset for too long. It wasn't in her. As I looked a Nika, I noticed Rachelle was sitting with the girl who wanted her ass whooped. As soon as she saw me, it was like my name was Casper, and she was a ghostbuster. I gave the bitch a couple of seconds to fully understand the ass whooping she was about to receive. At the time, I was so angry I just remember punching every piercing I saw on her face and slamming her into every ac transit seat around us. Even Nika after a certain point told me to please leave her alone, saying I got her good. I felt like I didn't get her enough, though, after all the shit this girl talked about me. I let that shit ride for a long time. I was fed up. I took her pack of cheap ass Tasha curls she got from Beauty Supply and told her they were mine. I wound up giving them back to her, but I was so mad. I wanted her to feel helpless and embarrassed like how she made others feel.

A lot of people in West Oakland are hard only because they are never alone. Everybody is a part of a family, so the bigger the pack, the greater the pride. But in this case, the bitch didn't have her fat cousin or other family around to protect her or to jump me. Rachelle, the twin, couldn't really do anything because it wasn't her fight. She wasn't the one talking shit. It was just instant karma. The bus driver called the police, but I was so mad I was going to beat that bitch's ass until the police got there, but Nika convinced me to run from the scene. I called my mom, and she picked me up in downtown Oakland, and we went to my granny's house for a little while. About fifteen minutes later, Major called me and said the same girls I fought before were talking shit and that the one bitch's face was all knotted up, but she wanted to fight me again. I knew exactly who it was, the same bitch I'd just beaten up, but now she had her people. She was ready. I didn't give a fuck at this point. I was going beat the fuck out of whomever again. My mom was hesitant to let me out of the car, but when we first pulled up, I bounced out. As soon as I did, she hopped in her the car, so I went up to the window where Major was talking to the girl's older sister. He explained we weren't about to keep going back and forth. I was there now if she wanted to fight. I was super calm. It was scary. That's how I knew I was ready. It took someone talking a lot of shit for someone to push me to that point. But I didn't like wasting energy arguing. I told the girl to come on and get it over with. I didn't know why she came back to my house. It was like she didn't learn that that pissed me off before. She had something on her face to take the swelling down. Neither she nor her cousin ever got out the car. She told me she would fight me another day. She was in too much pain to fight, I guess. Yet, this is the same person who came to my house because she felt the fight wasn't fair. I honestly felt like karma was a bitch, and she got what she had coming. They wound up driving off.

Chapter 11

I started to get really close to Tati, and we hung out every day after school. I always found my way over there. I was young but smart, and I stayed out of bullshit for the most part. I just was having trouble keeping up with everything and everyone else. My parents weren't aware of half of the things I had to do to make money. I was taught many different ways getting cash—everything from selling drugs to boosting clothes to milking different people out of shit to working in different programs if I were eligible. I was hustling good or bad, but I swear I tried to think of things that would not get me into too much trouble. I was getting a little money here and there, but not like I wanted. One day, I went over to Tati's house, but I only had a couple of dollars from cleaning my granny's house in Acorn. I had about ten dollars to spare. It was always lit over at Tati's granny's house. We always used to get hella high, but I tried to not be a burden on everyone as far as free loading, but weed was always around me. Everyone would contribute a bit, whether they had five dollars or twenty, but sometimes I would have to save my money for school, food, and getting on the bus. I came in and gave Nika the ten, so we could get some weed from the dealer, Big C.

Out of nowhere, one of Tati's cousins blatted out, "Yeah, Kasandra, we just knew you didn't have no money with yo broke ass."

It shocked me. I looked at her instantly kind of thrown off.

She looked back at me and calmly said, "Naw, am just playing."

There was silence like nobody knew what I was going to say after that, but I didn't make a big deal out of it. It did make me want to show older people around me I was mature, not just mentally but financially as well. It woke my game up to have somebody joking about my being broke and not having enough money to pitch in to get high. It definitely bugged me. I didn't like to be called broke, even if I was the youngest, so I started saving my money, and I started hanging out with my older cousin, Bev. She was my OG. A lot of people can say what they want about her, but at the end of the day, she would give you some real game that you should have been buying. Because she admired my maturity, she laced me up to the max. She taught me how to work tricks and get money out of a conversation. I really appreciated Bev. She taught a lot of the young girls how to get some money for real. Whether it was good or bad, she always acknowledged my potential. She always encouraged me to be better because she always told me to fuck those bitches who don't want anything in life. She saw that I did. She knew I was going to be great when I got older because I was hella solid.

Bev worked at the 99 Cent Store at the time, but she also sold dope and did hair. And even though she wanted to do her own thing, she still made sure she was good for a long. Bev and I would have talks about her wanting to just be free and do her own shit, and eventually that's what she did, and she was happy as fuck doing it. We would all meet up at Trisha's house because her dad worked a lot and let her have a lot of freedom. We used to hang out there in the village dancing, turning up, getting high. Some bitches in the hood made a fake online account making fun of other women. It had a lot of different people from West Oakland featured on it, but it had a couple of bitches from the Bottoms, too. One of the posts had Bev's picture, and it said she looked like LeBron James with that big ass forehead. I felt the bitch who made the account must have been miserable to make a post like that, especially when Bev was only about her money. I felt like she was just mad Bev was older and hanging out with younger girls, but I respect Bev for being around us. She loved me, and I felt she wanted to see me win, even if I wasn't making money with her. She knew I had it in me to be successful.

Back at MetWest, I was very social but also kept to myself at times. I can admit I was a real nerd. I got into an acting club for some extra credits and wound up really interested in acting. I loved playing a character and getting to be someone else. My acting coach's name was Eden. She was a Filipino lady and was really cool. I dove deeper into the program by joining a big play that was going to be produced by the Bay Arts Academy on Fruitvale. There I was, exposed to a whole new world of theater and art. It was a magical place for me. There were older people who worked for and participated in the play. I remember a couple of people's names, including Justin, Simone, and Malikia. We would all meet every week and practice the play coming up. There were many different messages within the play, and I liked the fact we could pick our own names and make up our own characters. My name was Amajah, my niece's name. Eden wanted us to really get into character so whatever talents we possessed, she integrated into the play. I chose to rap, and I remember working on my piece for about a month before I could get it right. I really wanted it to make sense and express how amazing I felt at that time. The rap went like this:

"Perfection is the limit. Gotta be past the illest. No sucker in my blood. Bring it from the realist. Taking it from respect, bringing it to the next. If you sugar coating shit, I'ma have to put you in check. Converting into a savage just to be living lavash. See you have some ideas here to bring the baggage. They stick to me like a magnets. I need, I gotta have it. Like a Knock with a pipe and a whole box of mavericks, I sit back, relax, and let life go on. I cherish a moment when it's gone, it's gone. Preparing me for the worst 'cause it will come unexpectedly. I thank God for living 'cause tomorrow's not promised to me. Cold hearted mind, so I don't have no sympathy. Thriving for the best. In my head it's a symphony. Gotta be somebody, so I challenge myself mentally."

If anger in the way, you can just call it physically Give me some room because it's time for me to come through have you really heard paralyze make you wanna sue it comes to me naturally you gotta get through the faculties I've been through some good and I've been through some tragedies ...

These verses meant so much to me. I was around fourteen when I created this piece. I thought so hard about how to put this together, and I studied it and rehearsed it for so long. Lyrics don't age, and that message applies still today. I really have to push to become a stronger version of myself.

I had a couple of friends at MetWest. Lee Lee Mabon had a lot of family from Oakland, and I went to school with her cousin Lilah and her sister. I actually dated her other cousin later on at the end of high school. My peer coach, who was my laughing partner, used to crack me up about the stupidest shit. He really got me into a lot of trouble because of how silly we used to be, and when we started getting high together, we really got into trouble. Sometimes I had to stop hanging out with him to push him. I know it sounds weird, but our advisor, Carolyn Nord was very passionate about our interests and how we were going to contribute to the world to make it better. I loved Carolyn. She was so disappointed in me when I fought that girl in class. I was going through so much, and I still don't like the girl for telling on me. The first year I went to MetWest, I almost got expelled from school because she told Carolyn we got high together.

My cousin Johnisha was in a grade above me, so I didn't spend too much time with her, but when we did get together, it was lit. Johnisha was half white and from a town called Hollister. She was not my blood cousin; however, it didn't matter. She was the reason I was at MetWest. My uncle Rashad encouraged my parents to send me there because I was too smart and was getting into too much trouble at McClymonds. MetWest was different and opened my eyes to life and to more people.

Once I developed a good schedule with going homework, interning, and getting high, I mastered school. I always completed my schoolwork and homework, and I started arriving on time and taking school more seriously because I was determined to go to college. I knew I had to have good grades if I wanted to go to an all-black school and become an actress or an athlete.

Chapter 12

Major came home from jail after his third time, and at this point I was into way more stuff than he knew about. He would try his hardest not to get into my business, but his instinct always made him go through my things eventually, but I was always a step ahead of him. Well, I tried to be. According to him, he was my big brother, and my business was his business until I showed him I could handle my own, but when he came home this time around, he could actually see I was pretty mature. We still used to bump heads a lot, but we were past all the fighting after he beat my ass in front of the whole hood. I wasn't about to keep fighting him, and he could no longer control me. He knew I was a young lady now, so he showed me respect to certain level. Plus, when he heard his little sister was beating bitches up while he wasn't around, he was forced to understand what I was about. I didn't want to fight bitches, but it was something I had to do to stay respected.

My brother never really put me in difficult situations unless he had to, and honestly, I didn't like fighting about bullshit. One day, my brother woke me up and told me some girl kept calling out his name. He had given her a lot of chances before he started to disrespect her. He explained to the girl that he, too, had a little sister. I was surprised because I had just gone out with that same girl the night before to some party. I didn't know if she knew that exactly or if she knew who I was when my brother told her, but my brother said she still didn't care, even after he told her to stop disrespecting him. My brother and I didn't always get along, but when it came down to it, I was there for him. I was always there, even when he didn't want me to be. I knew my brother only fucked with a few people from the Bottoms, and by this point, he'd outgrown some of them, or rather realized he was on another level and wanted to get to an even bigger level.

We walked all through the Bottoms to the end of the village because she was at Trisha's granny's house. I didn't do too much talking. I was honestly pissed off at the fact I was with the same girl the night before. I didn't want to fight her, but the fact that my brother woke me up out my sleep for this meant he was disrespected on another level. I knew my brother wasn't going to let a baby take his bottle. His pride wouldn't let anyone else win, but one thing I can say about my brother is he's not going to disrespect someone for no reason. My mom instilled in us to have manners, whether she was on one or not. She always made sure we acknowledged adults and weren't shit starters. I remember the girl was with Trisha and other cousins, who at the time knew her more than they knew me. They felt it was disrespectful for me to beat the girl up in front of their granny's house. But the cousins were talking shit only because she got her ass beaten. If she would have won the fight, it would have been another story, just like when those bitches showed up in front of my house wanting to fight.

In West Oakland, disrespectful people would cross boundaries and violate people's space to the max. That started to grow on me after I saw nobody had respect, but I apologized to granny after that. I was truly sorry, even though it was not in her house or anywhere near her. It was still out of character for me. I just remember dragging her from the porch to the street. I felt like she used granny's house as an escape and wanted me to get into it with everybody else, but all of them couldn't say shit to me. I didn't run into her house, and I didn't disrespect anybody who did not deserve it.

My brother had a friend named Grayson who worked with him at job core. He was chill and unbothered, didn't like drama, and had my brother's back, but Major found out really quickly who was on his level and who he wanted to hang around, and eventually Marcus became his go to. They started hanging together more often than real brothers. They built a bond and ran the 7th Street store.

There were a lot of bum bitches in disguise in West Oakland, and my brother asked me who was the rawest bitch I'd seen at the time. I was a young teenager still, so most of the old females were getting money in my eyes, but when I look back now, they only had enough to pay who they needed to. They didn't have a stable place to take care of their kids, let alone the energy to chase someone who really didn't want them. But my brother was big, and he wanted the baddest bitch down there. Truth be told, the hottest bitches were the most tarnished. He was going through it will Audrianna, yet he still wanted to be a dad to my niece who was about three. It seemed like the streets were pulling him in more and more, or he allowed his ego to take over because he had a point to prove. He wasn't from any part of West Oakland, yet his family stayed down here. He was going back and forth between Sunnyside and the Bottoms. A lot of guys hated that, while others had to respect it.

Out of all the bitches in the Bottoms, there were few I thought Major could hit it off with because nobody really knew him, but all of that changed really fast as soon as he walked to the store. That walk to 8th Street store was either going to make him or break him. I told Major he couldn't get Nika, but he said he'd been seeing her and was waiting for the right time to approach her. She was officially trying to get out of the relationship she was in, and for whatever reason Nika started to open up more and go out with us more often. Her boyfriend did not like this at all, but Nika started to live her best life. We would handle our business, make our little money together, get our hair done together, get dressed us together, and chill together. We were a vibe, and Nika would wear heels through the whole hood. I don't know how she did it, but she did it with a beautiful smile, too.

Chapter 13

At this point, I was pretty much known in the Bottoms. I was a chill, but fun person and always tried to look out for people even if they wronged me. In West Oakland, anything can happen at any time. That was one of the scariest things about living in West Oakland. I never knew when something was going to happen, but I knew it was going to happen, and when it did, it was going to be really ugly. There was everything from people getting robbed to bitches getting beat up by their boyfriends to drive by shootings to stabbings to drug busts to cousins killing each other. I used to go around the Bottoms when Keola was doing something or I saw what Jayauna and Makiara were up to. If I couldn't find them, I would see what Tati and that crew was doing. There were some days we all be together getting high, dancing, and talking shit. There was some fake shit going on, but if any outsiders tried to fuck with one of us, we would all come together.

As Nika started to hang with us more often—something I thought she'd never do because she was really reserved—Tati started getting out more. I really wasn't trying to be around Major for many reasons at this time since he'd been distancing himself from the family. He had this money-making mentality, and Lord knows what else he was going through. My mom was very irritable at this time, and asking my dad for anything wasn't an option. I also hated to ask my mom for things because I had to wait on her for even ten dollars. She always paid everybody she owed except her kids. We always had to wait, but my mom always made up for it, meaning she came through when she really needed to. At this point, I learned nobody asked to be crackhead or a bum, and my mom always made sure we had enough, and I really appreciate that about her. I never felt unsafe in my home nor was I scared. However, there was a lot of dysfunction I knew wasn't okay.

I started having these nightmares, and they became a pattern. It's like I could tell something was about to happen. In my dream, I would hear gunshots and my mama crying. She would be screaming, "My baby! My baby!" I had many dreams, but not many about gun violence. They always involved something I'd seen on TV, like Chucky or a leprechaun, never my mama crying and screaming to her baby. I started to reflect on all the things I did and all the people I hurt. I asked God to forgive all my sins, and I thanked him for allowing me to still have all my brothers in my life despite living in a society that set them up to fail. As a black person, it is so hard to be successful, but I feel that it is a mentality we have to fight in order to overcome the barriers. Life is what we make it. If you understand the odds are formed against you, you know what not to become. A lot of people think that dying with pride for their street or their gang is enough, but that is what the oppressors want.

There was so much shit going on in West Oakland. There was a murder scene every week from Ghost Town to Dog Town, to Berkeley back to the Bottoms and through Cypress to Acorn. The whole of West Oakland was becoming unsafe, and people were dropping like flies. It was a matter of time before something was going to hit home. I felt it. Seeing Keola lose her brother Keylow was horrific. I could only imagine what she was going through. She, too, had a lot of brothers, and she and Keylow were really close in age like Ray Ray and me. I kept thinking about my nightmares and what they meant.

One day, I got a call that Jayauna's brother and a couple of his friends were shot by a gang. They had been drinking in their area of the Bottoms, and the people targeted by this violence were not actually affiliated with any gang. I knew one of the young boys who was shot in his eye socket and almost died. He is a survivor, who is now thriving and not letting his disability hold him back. He has so much hope for his future, even though the doctor said he wasn't going to make it. He said otherwise. This incident traumatized my community and the people close to me. At this point, I thought of these people as family. I cared so much for them, and I felt our ancestors lived and fought so we could breathe and be the best we could be.

It got so bad, I started staying indoors as much as possible. It wasn't safe. It was murder season when gangs go on killing sprees, murdering anybody just so they can put it in their next song. They were keeping score between them—a body for a body. Gangs that were clicked up started to fall out. People started to backdoor each other. There was some really snake shit going on. You may wonder how I knew all of this, how I knew how it really was, and believe it or not, a lot of the factual information was coming from the bitches the gang members were fucking. It was so bad, even my parents were aware of the shootings that were happening back-to-back. At that point, my parents and I had a better understanding. They knew I was just going to rebel, but I was fifteen or sixteen, and I was becoming more responsible. My mom always asked me to just never lie to her, to always tell her where I was, though it was better for her to not know exactly where I was most of the time. She would have had a heart attack knowing I was out there popping pills and having sex at a young age. My mom told me stories of her childhood and how she grew up not having much of one. I felt so sad for my mom, and the older I get, the more I realize she was a motherless child who just wanted real love, and her kids gave her that. I know I stress my mom out the most, but it's because I see her potential. She is so loving and firm like a Madea. She gives us that old fashioned love.

On Major's twenty-first birthday, we threw him a small party. Some of my friends were around, and we had cake and dinner. My dad was drunk, and he started to get loud with my brother. Major was trying to be as respectful as he could be, but I could tell he couldn't take any more. He and my dad started tussling all the way down the stairs and outside. I was trying to break it up the whole time, but somehow while trying to break them up, my dad uppercut me on accident. I didn't feel anything, and he didn't do it on purpose, but I think he was responsible because he shouldn't have gotten overly drunk. Major was tired of all the drunk shit. After all, he was turning twenty-one. At this point, my brother had gone to jail for a few different crimes on a level my dad wanted no part of. Major was trying his hardest to not go there with my dad, but I felt like my dad was asking for it. He started having a tantrum like child. He got so drunk, he started repeating the same thing over and over and got angry, but on this particular day, my brother had a rage bigger than my dad's. I always felt like Major didn't like me because my dad would chastise him, but none of that mattered to Major on this day. He was determined to show my dad that a lot of his shit was not about to keep happening. Major even patted on my mama's pussy, telling my dad that that was his.

When my dad accidentally knocked me out, I went into a seizure. I woke to my dad shaking me and hugging me and asking if I was okay. I just remember screaming at him, asking why he hit me. I could tell my dad was really drunk and disappointed in himself, but he didn't show it. Only when he went overboard he would apologize. I remember the ambulance coming and asking my mom if she wanted me to go to the hospital. I said no because I wanted to stay back and make sure my family didn't fight. After getting knocked out by my own dad, I still stayed thinking it was going to calm everybody down, but this distanced my brother even more.

My mom just let shit ride out thinking in time it would get better, but I felt like this was the beginning of all of her kids not going for my daddy's drunk shit anymore. As children, we respected him because he was our dad, but I lost a lot of respect for my dad when I felt he was causing harm to our family. Instead of providing and handling business, he started drinking more causing my mom to hold down the rent and juggle the needs for all of us kids by herself. My mom had a warrant out for her arrest, so she didn't like driving. My dad took us places in his pickup truck or rode his bike everywhere. I did not like when he used to pull up on me on his bike in front of my friends because that shit used to be so embarrassing. The fact he thought that at forty-five years old it was okay to recycle and collect metal for change killed me. He did not want to work back at the Marriott because he didn't want to stop drinking. I felt bad for my mom, but I was also mad at her for allowing someone to bring down our family. I get that was her husband, but to allow him to sabotage his family in this way was disappointing.

My dad would have temper tantrums when he didn't get what he wanted, whether it was crack, a beer, or even pussy from my mom. He would brake things and say the same thing over and over again, then go to the store to get another bottle of vodka. He would drink so much he had to force himself to throw up. I would hear him almost every night. It was routine. He would come out of the bathroom teary-eyed and have the nerves to keep drinking. I knew my dad was going through a lot; I just wished he would have slowed down drinking and paid attention to our needs more. I wish he were a provider. I appreciate my dad for teaching me about nature and challenging my physical abilities. I loved showing my dad how smart I was because I wanted him to see how intellectual I was. I could comprehend things on a whole other level. I loved comparing and contrasting things at a young age and asking questions when I was curious. The biggest thing I thank my dad for is staying in my life, whether it was for his comfort or because he really wanted his many children to have a dad didn't matter. Honestly, I couldn't imagine not having my dad around even if he was a drunk and took his anger out on us at times. He always was around. I believe he tried, but I don't believe he tried hard enough when it came down to teaching me what a man is supposed to do for his family and his wife. I understood later that you cannot force someone to see their own potential. All you can do is be the best version of yourself and hope you motivate them. By the time I was sixteen years old, a full-blown teenager, I had gone through so much with my parents— everything from lying to sneaking out to smoking to boys to parties to gangs. I was very mature and had started to communicate with my mom more. I was tired of lying and hiding things from her. She started allowing me to have more freedom, even letting me take my little brother Ray Ray to more parties and functions. It was grimy outside for a whole year. There were off and on shootings in West Oakland, so my mom tried to keep us in the house, but it got to the point where I just wanted to get high and not fuck up her own because I was bored in the house. Eventually she felt bad and let us go out to parties or to our friends' homes.

Chapter 14

On the sixth of November in 2011, I was cooking breakfast for my mom. I remember making a good ass breakfast that day. Everything felt great, and my mom and I weren't arguing. I got cleaned up and was about to start my day, but as I was bringing my mom her breakfast plate with bacon, eggs, buttered toast, and potatoes, she got a call. I knew something was wrong because my mom had this look on her face I'd never seen before. It was like she was frozen for a couple of seconds. She dropped her plate, and all her food fell to the floor. She started yelling and screaming at the top of her lungs. She bounced up and started looking around. I knew something wasn't right, but at this point, I was in shock. I immediately thought somebody had died, so I started looking for all my brothers. My heart dropped down into my stomach. I looked in each room. Greg was in jail, so I immediately thought Major was killed, but Major came out the room wanting to know what was going on. The call my mom received was a restricted call. The man on the other line said, "Ma'am, I hate to be the bearer of bad news, but your son Kenny has been shot on 10th and Peralta."

At that moment, we were all hysterical. As soon as Major heard 10th and Peralta, he ran out the door. I grabbed my mom's keys as my whole family rushed out after him. I only had a robe and some underwear on. It's sad to say, but I remember the day Ray Ray got shot very well. It's almost like it plays out in slow motion even to this day. The nightmares I'd been having came true. In my dream, I didn't think it was Ray Ray my mom was crying over, but I guess it was that whole time—Ray Ray, my sweet little boy! Kenny Ray, who was fourteen years old, was shot while walking home from his friend's house where he'd stayed the night.

My granny happened to be calling my mom in the midst of our arriving to the scene. I remember hovering around Ray Ray. He looked lifeless at first, but as I got closer, I saw he was calm. It looked like he couldn't move. He was talking very slowly to all of us, telling us he was okay and that he was trying to stay calm. I was hysterical. I kept screaming out to him that I loved him, to please hold on because the ambulance was on the way. I remember Ray Ray holding my dad's hand. I couldn't take seeing my brother so lifeless, so I started yelling at the police, asking them where the fuck medical attention was and begging them to find the people responsible for this violence. Major picked me up and put me in the back seat of my mom's car. I started fighting with him because I was so out of it. I wanted to stay with Ray Ray, but I was way too emotional at the time, and he needed peace. He was so calm. Just imagine getting shot ten times and being conscious enough to tell someone to call your mom at fourteen years old. Incredible.

My grandmother pulled up before the ambulance did. As a matter of fact, it took the ambulance thirty-five minutes to get my brother off the ground. Thank God he was calm, and he didn't bleed out too fast. He also did not get hit in any of his main arteries. I was out of it. I wanted it to wake up from this nightmare. I asked God why him? I wanted it to be me instead. It was so painful to see my baby brother in such a state. Before Major grabbed me, I remember I kept telling Ray Ray how much I loved him. I kept asking God to keep him. Ray Ray told us it was going to be okay. After everything he was going through, he still tried to stay humble and positive. I remember people coming from around the neighborhood, and the crowd grew bigger and bigger as we waited for the ambulance to get there. I cannot even describe the pain I was feeling at the time. I was in utter shock. It felt like I was dying emotionally. My soul was pouring out crying to God in way I had never imagined possible. My whole family experienced this traumatic event, from the oldest, my grandmother Sandra Toliver, at sixty-one to the youngest, Keshad, who was only ten. I can't imagine what my parents felt seeing their child lying on the ground unable to get up because he was shot ten times with two different guns, a 9mm pistol and a Glock 40, and not knowing if this was the last time they would see their child alive. The men responsible didn't know who they were shooting. Shooting random children isn't gangster at all.

The ambulance took so long we were considering taking Ray Ray to the hospital ourselves, but he said he couldn't walk and he couldn't feel his legs. I already knew he couldn't walk by how his body was positioned on the ground when we first saw him. When the ambulance finally came, we followed it to Highland Hospital where Ray Ray went into emergency surgery. He was in the operating room for at least five hours. My granny had given me a Valium to calm my nerves. It was my first time taking that, but I honestly needed it, even though I threw it up about fifteen minutes later. My nerves were so bad after I threw up, I went to sleep hoping that day would end.

KASANDRA JOHNSON

I woke up to the revelation that the nightmare was reality. My brother was shot ten times. I was so sick day in and day out, but God gave me the strength to push through and nurture him back to health with the help of my family. I would like to leave you all with this piece I wrote for my people who grew up in depressed areas or inner cities.

"Stop The Violence"
Let's stop the violence, love our people
Gotta stay strong
Our people dying, steady crying
Gotta hold on and no denying
Our mommas gotta pray strong
'Cause evil's watching, tryna take you out your safe zone
The streets getting lethal
Time to rise up and be the voice for me and my people
Oppression real, I know how you feel
Risking yo life for a meal
Just have some hope
They threw us the rope
Thinking we're all going to choke, but we came on that boat
As king and queens, just know we ain't no joke
We cream of the crop, forever on top, society saying we not
But we gotta stop believing lies, so we can make it to the top
When it's gonna stop
We live in streets where kids and babies popped
It's been a lot, it's sad to say
Used to the sound of a Glock.
Just listen...
Understand that society paints you out to be victims.
Did I mention they keep us trapped?
Can't go out of jurisdiction
They on a mission
It's their intention, they say that we fit the discrimination
So be attentive, have faith, and hold on as God as my witness
Just look how we living
We cook dope and sell it like we fried chicken straight out the kitchen

THE STRUGGLE THAT MADE ME

We live by the gun and kill when we in are feelings
I hope you feel this 'cause this some real shit
And we really live it
We got the ticket, our melon is priceless
Worth more than millions, and that's why they fear us
They know the real us
It's time to reveal us
We are some leaders, we our own teachers, it's skin deeper
We are keepers, and to my brothers, I am the grim reaper
And it's skin deeper, we are our teachers, we are some leaders.

ABOUT THE AUTHOR

Kasandra Johnson hails from Oakland, where she discovered a sense of purpose and a unique connection to others. Growing up amidst adversity, she embarked on a journey of self-discovery at a young age and developed a keen awareness of life's challenges.

Driven by a deep spiritual connection to her ancestors and a passion for music, Kasandra found moments of clarity and liberation. Music served as both a guide and a refuge, and she emerged with a heightened awareness and a profound sense of responsibility for her own life and the lives of her loved ones. Having witnessed firsthand the ravages of drugs, mental health struggles, dysfunctional environments, and the specter of violence that looms large in her community, she persevered, grappling with her own demons while striving to break free from the cycles of generational trauma.

Today, Kasandra channels her experiences into a mission of healing and empowerment, offering strategies for liberation and growth to others facing similar challenges. Her story is one of resilience and determination, a testament to the human spirit capacity to overcome adversity and strive for a better future.

Made in the USA
Columbia, SC
01 September 2024

898bb917-7450-4d66-af39-c5efb78f8eb7R01